PLANETCASH.com !

CASH FLOW
AND
BEYOND

C.A. QM-17

CASH FLOW AND BEYOND

A collection of wisdom and formulas for increasing cash flow, protecting assets, enhancing wealth, preparing for a great retirement and bequeathing to loved ones all you've worked for.

WADE B. COOK

With J.J. Childers, John Hudelson, Steve Wirrick
and Greg Witt

Wade Cook Seminars, Inc.
A subsidiary of Wade Cook Financial Corporation
A publicly traded corporation
Ticker symbol: WADE
Seattle, Washington

Distributed to the trade by
Origin Books, Inc.

This publication is designed to provide accurate and authoritative information in regard to the subject matter covered. It is sold with the understanding that the publisher is not engaged in rendering legal, accounting, or other professional service. If legal or expert assistance is required, the services of a competent professional person should be sought.

From a declaration of principles jointly adopted by a committee of the American Bar Association and committee of the Publishers Association.

Cover Photo by Zac Cherry
Cover Design by Angie Wilson
Layout by Matt Krein
Art Direction by Mark Engelbrecht
These chapters are excerpted
from various books published by
Lighthouse Publishing Group, Inc.
14675 Interurban Avenue South
Seattle, Washington 98168-4664

Printed in the USA   Second edition
10 9 8 7 6 5 4 3 2

CASH FLOW AND BEYOND
Table Of Contents

Introduction

CASH FLOW:
"The pattern of cash income and expenditures of a person or business, and the resulting availability of cash.

– Wade B. Cook, Brilliant Deductions

Cash flow is something we are all concerned with, whether we know the term or not. Cash flow determines the amount of cash in your pocket or bank account, whether your family lives the way you'd like them to, and whether you are as free as you dream of being. Cash flow is the key to your financial life, and you may not even be aware of it.

This is the story of Wade "Cash Flow" Cook and his publicly traded company, Wade Cook Financial Corporation (ticker symbol:WADE). You'll find as you go along that it's a classic tale of an ordinary man who dreamed of building financial security for his family. As you read his story and the excerpts in this book you will begin to see the cash flow principles and formulas that took a cab driver from Tacoma, Washington to the halls of high finance on Wall Street. Wade Cook the taxi driver now drives a Bentley because of what he learned about creating and maintaining cash flow. He can teach it to you and show you how to use that knowledge to achieve your dreams.

The excerpts you'll find here are from books by Wade Cook and other authors published by Lighthouse Publishing Group, Inc., a Wade Cook Financial Corporation subsidiary. Lighthouse Publishing scours the country for the best and brightest of financial minds and works with them to develop materials that teach you and train you to reach your financial goals. Whether you currently drive a Ford or a Ferrari, you can move to another level by learning from these extraordinary people. Climb in behind Wade Cook and ride along-you'll be surprised by the journey!

SECTION 1

The Dream

Once upon a time a man had a business that taught people how to make money in the stock market. Here's how it started:

A friend, a stockbroker, came to him with a proposal—a proposal to buy a certain stock with the intention of selling it for a small profit rather than hanging onto it for years in hopes of a big increase down the line. This plan sounded remarkably similar to a real estate concept called the Money Machine he had already made successful (but more on that later). He followed his friend's advice, wondering and watching to see if the same principles that had worked in cab driving and real estate could possibly hold true in the stock market.

After several rounds of buying and selling this stock, the man believed he had found a way to make the kind of money he was interested in. His experience in real estate, however, taught him that true success, ongoing success, teachable success, depends on a formula that is repeatable, so he began to study this stock and others to see if they could be played the same way. When he was done, he had discovered a remarkable opportunity, something he called Rolling Stock...

The more he studied the stock market, the more the man found other formulas that could be used for a Wall Street Money Machine: Bottom Fishing, Stock Splits, Option Strategies, and more. In radio interviews and his real estate seminars he started asking people if they were interested in hearing about his discoveries. The response was overwhelmingly positive, and the Wall Street Workshop seminar was born...

Well, the man started to teach these strategies. He saw many, many people come to his Wall Street Workshop and succeed beyond their wildest dreams using the training he offered. Again, people retired, spent more time with their loved ones, adopted long-wanted children, and contributed to churches and charities with the money and time made available by the Money Machine.

(Continued on page 15)

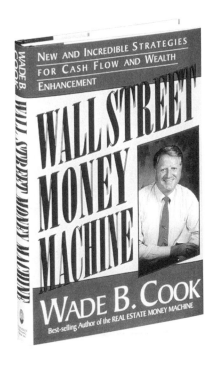

3

Making Your Money Work Hard

Rate Of Return

I have repeatedly espoused this formula in my major course, the *Wall Street Workshop* and in my *Stock Market Home Study Course*. I am convinced that many people do not know how to make a lot of money because they don't know how to measure the effectiveness of their money. I am talking about calculating a simple yield or a "rate of return."

It is really quite simple. To figure your rate of return, take the money that you get back from a particular investment and divide it by the cash you have tied up in the investment. In real estate and other forms of tax shelter investments, you would calculate the cash you get back in the form of income, and you could also calculate the increase in the value of the property and tax savings you receive. You could spend a lot of time calculating specific rates of return based on different features of an investment.

When it comes to stock market investments, I am particularly interested in the cash-on-cash yield. I am not looking at a compounding yield, except as a fun figure to calculate from time to time. An actual cash-on-cash yield is measured by taking the cash that I get back on an investment and dividing it by the money I have tied up.

The only concern I have is this: when most people calculate yields, they have a tendency to calculate them on an annualized basis. For example, if you had $10,000 in a CD earning 5%, at the end of the year you would have $500 or possibly $540 in compounded interest. That would be the yield: 5% or 5.4%.

When it comes to stock market investments, use my formulas and you will notice that I do a lot of things in two-week to one-month periods. For example, I usually write covered calls for the next month out. I am generating one-month premiums or one- and two-week premiums. My rate of return then is a one-month rate of return, which is substantially different from an annualized return.

If you wanted to calculate an annualized return, you could take a one-month return and multiply by 12, or take a two-week return and multiply by 26 (there are 26 two-week periods in a year.) If you start thinking in terms of monthly returns and going after investments that produce large two- and four-week returns, then the whole nature of your cash flow and the volume of your cash flow will substantially change. The point is, figure out how much you are getting back for every dollar you invest.

Spend Profits, Not Principal

One of the earliest pieces of advice I learned when I started investing money was to spend my profits, not my principal. Let me relate that to using the money you are making in your brokerage account. Most of you, in setting up your brokerage accounts, will have all of the money going back into different investments. At some point, though, the needs in your life will change. You will need to start living off the income from your investments. But until that point, let me share some ideas you can apply with the profits from dividends, capital gains, or income.

You can immediately plow money back into stock. If you have a stock that has a "dividend reinvestment program," you definitely should take advantage of it. You will be able to buy additional shares of stock in the company with these dividends and without paying any commissions. Sometimes you can buy the stock at a 10% discount (so all of your money at a discount is going back into the stock).

One of the best newsletters in the country for learning more about this is called *The Money Paper.* Check the recommended reading section at the back of this book for more information on this paper. This newsletter will give you names of companies and even, for a small fee, sell you a single share from one of these companies, so that as a current stockholder you can get in on its dividend reinvestment program.

When I buy a new stock for the first time, my brokers tell me if it has a dividend reinvestment program attached to it. If it does, the brokers set up their computer so that each time a dividend is paid, it goes to buy more stock in the company.

The dividend may be paid while the stock price is high. If you are doing rolling stock with this company, that could be a little uncomfortable, but not too bad. In lieu of doing it that way, you could just have the dividends paid directly to your account or even have a check sent to your home.

Let me say it one more time: spend your profits, not your principal. Another way of saying this is to spend your interest, not your capital. Leave your capital base intact. Use it to spin off income to live on.

Bet On The Jockey

One concept that will always prove successful in investing is simply this: Bet on the jockey, not on the horse.

TEAM		PRODUCT	=	RESULTS
C	+	A	=	C+
A	+	C	=	A
A	+	A	=	A+

You see, if a company has a really good product (let's say an "A" product), but you have a "C" team of mediocre people handling the product, then you are going to have mediocre results. Conversely, if you have an "A" team, a really great group of people running the company or investment idea, even though the product or project may be a "C", the team will be successful, either bringing the "C" product to its potential or dumping it and finding other products. They will win.

When looking at investing in an apartment complex or other project through a limited partnership, look at the people handling it. What is their experience? How long have they been in the business? What other success stories have they had? What have their failures been? It is the quality of people that will determine the outcome of the company. Another way of looking at this is to learn from an old statement that my father made to me. He said, "Wade, if you are not going to be a star yourself, latch onto a star."

What Drives A Stock Up?

I like to find stocks that are going to have a lot of upward pressure. I remember when I was driving a taxi, from time to time I would see a Plymouth Fury in the garage. We had a few small cars, like Dodge Darts, but most of our cabs were Plymouth Furies. I knew the engines in these Chrysler products would last forever, if the right cars were purchased and taken care of.

The mechanics knew this too. Sometimes the Furies would have bald tires or the interiors would be torn up. Sometimes the paint job would look shabby, but rather than doing the little patch–up work on the exterior, the mechanics brought the cars in to check out the engine pressure.

That seemed to be all they were concerned with: the pressure of the engine. Individual car owners would be concerned about the look of the car, but not them. Engine pressure determined how long the cars would last and how much power they'd have.

How do we apply this to the stock market? I like to buy stocks in companies that have a good chance of going up. Call this the "pressure"—a lot of upside potential. It could be in either a sector or an industry group, or it could be a stock coming out of bankruptcy. New ideas, technology, new applications, mergers and acquisitions, stock splits, and new management all can provide pressure to drive the price up.

This pressure applies particularly well to turnaround candidates, stocks that have been in decline but show signs of charging forward again. Let me show you how to find them and gauge their potential.

Look in the newspaper, going down the left column of the stock page, and look at the highs and lows for the year. If you see a company's high for the year at $15 and a low at $13, and the stock is currently trading at $13.50, there is hardly any upward potential. Don't get me wrong—this stock could go from $13 up to $30 or $50 a share, but move on down the page and find this: a stock with a high of $13.00 but a low of $1 and currently trading at $1.50.

Now this company could be heading for bankruptcy and the stock could stop trading in a very short time, but at least you know there is turnaround potential. Don't think that just because you bought it at $1.50, it is going to go up. All you really know is that there has been something wrong with this company and it's a good time to do your homework.

Quick note: In the stock market pages, a small "vj" in front of the company name signifies that the company is in bankruptcy. (Please read under the Rolling Stock chapter about bankrupt companies.) Again, all that you learn here is that it is a turnaround candidate. Now it's time for you or your stockbroker to do your homework and find out if this company can come back out of the doldrums.

What can cause it to rise? 1) A change of management; 2) new licenses or applications of existing products; and 3) mergers with other companies. I like these kinds of companies because a lot of people have given up on them. (Remember the old stockholders who bought the stock at $12.00 or $13.00 a share and then watched it plummet.)

Some of these previous stockholders sold out at $8, some at $6, some at $4 and now the stock is clear down to $1 a share. Ask yourself, do these people want to get involved again? The answer is usually no. But those of us coming in new see the company and its turnaround potential. This presents a great way to find stocks, through a procedure I call "bottom fishing."

Bottom Fishing

Last fall my children and I stopped by a nursery and purchased some daffodil bulbs. Daffodils are one of my favorite flowers. Since I come from the Northwest, you can see why. We are famous for our daffodils up here. In Southern California they have the Rose Parade, and we have the Daffodil Parade here.

We took some time and dug our holes and planted the bulbs in the ground. Once we filled in the holes with dirt, my children stood back and immediately wanted to see the flowers. I had to explain to them that the flowers would not come out until after the winter. In the spring they would start to grow. I am confident that when spring comes and they see the results of their work and realize how beautiful the daffodils are, they will be as excited as can be.

When I talk about bottom fishing—buying low-priced stocks with the hope that the company will either turn around or grow in value—this is what we are hoping for. Plant the bulbs, and if you have good fertilizer, good soil, the right amount of water, the right kind of bulb, and a little luck, you will get the results you wished for. Not all the bulbs will grow, but I am confident that the few that grow and bloom will make a big difference in my stock portfolio.

Types Of Brokerage Accounts

When you go to open your brokerage account, you must realize there are three different types of firms. The information here will help you make a decision on which type of account or accounts to have.

The first type of account would be at a "full-service broker," including some of the largest and oldest brokerage houses: Merrill Lynch, Smith Barney, Piper Jaffray, etc. These brokerage houses will charge larger commissions, but they will also give you research data and reports and make a lot of information available to you. They will call you when they have a good deal.

The second type of brokerage account is with what is called a "discount broker." In this category, I would place Charles Schwab, Fidelity Investments, etc. They are about mid-range on the scale. I particularly like Charles Schwab, and I have many accounts there. Very user friendly, Charles Schwab has a computer tie-in service called "Street Smart" that lets me become a stockbroker at home. Because of my volume of trades, I have become a member of the Schwab 500 Team Club. Now I am able to get additional benefits.

The third type of broker is called a "deep-discount broker."

You cannot open up a financial magazine or any other financial paper without seeing several of these firms advertised. Falling into this category would be Accutrade, National Discount Brokers, Jack Smith & Co., Kennedy Cabot and a host of others. Their commissions are as low as $25 per trade, and sometimes it doesn't matter how much stock you trade.

One strategy I have a hard time agreeing with is to use all the information you get from a full-service broker and handle all your trades with a deep-discount broker. I don't like ripping off ideas like that.

Let me tell you what I did. I found a full-service broker because I like doing business with them, and their services are quite extensive and rewarding. The extra commissions I pay have more than been returned to me in terms of information I have learned about companies and investment strategies.

I have even moved some of my accounts to the full-service broker from the other types of brokers. First, I negotiated for the lowest possible commissions I could get. Don't think you need to have a lot of money to do this. I only put in around $5,000 to open the account. Obviously, the broker was hoping I'd recommend him to others. He gave me a discount rate of 40% off the standard rate after further negotiation. Request the "investment club" discount from your broker. (Note: I am not a broker and do not ever make recommendations, nor do I ever get anything when my students make trades through their brokers.)

You can have accounts at all three types of brokerage houses or just choose one that you like. It depends on your level of expertise and how much research you want to do. Remember, the deep-discount brokers and many discount brokers will not give you any advice at all. When I mention something to Charles Schwab brokers on the phone, there is complete silence, even if it's something simple like, "Well, I bought this stock at $3.50 and I am going to sell it again at $8.50. That's a $5 profit." They do not respond at all.

So, if you need to have a response, if you need ideas, if you need a sounding board, then you may want to consider a full-service broker. While I may not agree with that advice at all times, at least my full-service broker is there and I can use him as a sounding board for what I want to do.

Wall Street Money Machine is the book that has set the standard of stock market trading methods for the next century. Don't miss out on your opportunity to take advantage of the exciting "live version" taught at our *Wall Street Workshop*. Call **1-800-872-7411** today to find out if you are eligible for special discounts. Classes fill up fast and seating is limited!

Table Of Contents
from "Wall Street Money Machine"

The thanks and testimonials poured in. The man's courses became so popular that he could not keep up with the demand. He needed to train more teachers to help him lead the courses and hire customer service representatives to help the students wanting to register. He even had to develop an additional course-the Next Step Workshop-for people who wished to go beyond what they had learned at the Wall Street Workshop.

In the midst of his growing success with his courses, tapes and books, he began to see another part of the pattern repeated. Some people came to the Wall Street Workshop and did not succeed, either because they did not follow the formulas as they were taught or because they did not apply what they learned. There were even people who did not want to learn that they could achieve their dreams right then and there by using the stock market formulas.

In talking to these people he found that some were afraid to think about getting into the stock market. For years they had been reading opinions from this and that pundit warning that the current rising market (known as a "bull market") is due for a crash. Time and time again he spoke to people about the reasons for getting into stocks, only to run into this idea that the market will head down soon.

(*Continued on page 39*)

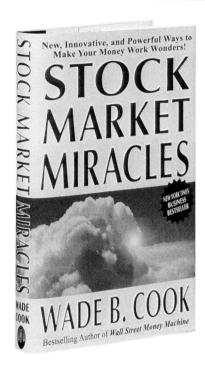

1

BUILDING A GREAT PORTFOLIO

When my first book on stock market investing hit the street, I was overwhelmed by the incredibly favorable response. I received countless letters and e-mail messages. These were no ordinary "thank yous," as most had included specific trades they had made, records of deals, and cash flow profits to be proud of. *"I've made $43,000 in one month," "$19,000 in three days," "We just adopted kids with the $30,000 we made this month."* Too many wonderful stories to mention here. See the testimonials at the beginning of the book for a sampling of the many exciting stories we hear.

But there have been the critics also. Don't misunderstand. I've not been criticized by anyone who actually read the book, and surely not by anyone who has followed the formulas and done the trades. Actually, the only real criticism has come from comments made on the jacket; like *"outrageous returns,"* or *"double your money every 2½ to 4 months."*

USING OPTIONS TO BUILD A PORTFOLIO

So to answer this light and superfluous charge, I dedicate this chapter to building a strong portfolio for the long term. I won't turn on my cash flow formulas. In fact, I'll use them to build a portfolio to be proud of—an "investment club" style portfolio, but I'll do so my way; defining the methods and even the terms, such as "long term."

I am no different than most prudent investors or pension and mutual fund managers. I want to look at my portfolio and see huge, brand-name stocks like AT&T, Boeing, Wrigley, McDonalds, Nordstrom, Sears, General Electric, Pfizer, Marriott, et cetera. I want to own stock in companies I can eat in, shop at, dial up, and sleep in! I like quality. I repeat, I like great companies with excellent growth, trademarks, earnings, market niche, and sheer strength of size. I want millions of dollars of them and I don't want to have to work a 9 to 5 job to get them. Boy, that's a conundrum. It's almost impossible to work a typical American job, with average income and accumulate millions. Yes, in 40 to 50 years maybe, but who wants to wait that long? That's the rub—accomplishing the task of having millions, without having to work for millions. So, it is not my goal or objective which differs from the "conventional wisdom" reeking from virtually every financial planner/stockbroker—the so-called experts—but the method of getting there. This is where we part ways.

You see, my method is simple. I want to use a small amount of money—risk capital if you will, to generate cash flow which will exponentially generate more income. I've never advocated that a person put his portfolio at risk with aggressive plays. In fact I've repeatedly and strongly advised against it.

To prove this point, and so there is no misunderstanding, I'll repeat it here. Use a small amount of money—say $2,000 to $10,000— to build a cash flow machine. Keep the balance of your money in high grade stocks, bonds, mutual funds, and even in real estate and other businesses outside the traditional stock market investments. The stock market is simply too risky for me.

Will Rogers said it best: "I'm worried about the return *of* my money, not just the return *on* it."

Let's deal with the $2,000 to $10,000 figures. That may seem high to participants of the "meet the 2nd Tuesday of each month, invest $50 a month and sit around for hours discussing one or two stocks, and hope for the best" clubs so prevalent today. Let's break everyone into categories: those with *under $100,000* to invest, and those with *over $100,000* to invest. Everyone reading this falls into one of these two categories. That's simple, but the next part is not so simple. If you only have $2,000 or so to get started, then I'll make an assumption—your family is young. If you're older, (say older than 40) and you can barely scrape together $2,000, then you probably need a different book than this one—perhaps a motivational book, or one on vitamin pills. Whatever, young or old, if that's it, then find the most outrageous, crazy, wild, risky plan you can find and go for the gusto. What do you have to lose? Surely you can get back (earn, et cetera) $2,000 to $5,000. In Arizona, they teach you that if you have water (bottle, canteen, et cetera) and you get stranded in the desert — drink it all—now! Apparently our bodies store and ration liquids better than our minds.

If you have $100,000, then take $95,000 and buy safe, secure, blue chip, "hold for the long term" stocks. Be extra safe. Now take $2,000 to $5,000 and go to town. Treat the stock market like a business. Be aggressive.

Read the following letter and see what I mean. The last time I talked to this man, his $20,000 was over $267,000 and that's three to four months after attending my Wall Street Workshop. He's on target to make over $1,000,000 in one year, from his $20,000.

Dear Mr. Cook,

Enclosed please find a copy of my extended resume and a video copy of my film product reel. No, I'm not looking for employment, I've included it so that you can see that my occupation is not one conducive to "playing the stock market." I'm a movie maker. I write, direct, and produce features for theatre and television.

Pretty far removed from the market, wouldn't you say? So, why am I sending it? For one reason . . . I'm now six weeks or so past one of your Houston Wall Street Workshops and the results have been interesting (an understatement)!

As a filmmaker, I move from project to project. I've just completed a two-hour television special entitled, America, A Call To Greatness *with Charlton Heston, Mickey Rooney, Deborah Winters, and Peter Graves. Next week, I'll be directing several episodes of a new fall series for ABC. In between, I do nothing. It's these periods of inactivity that annoy me. It's not that I have to be constantly active, but it helps. In my industry, these periods are referred to as "being between pictures." Translated, it means unemployed—"waiting." I've been in the industry for some years and I always have work . . . and I always have inactivity. Having heard of your workshop, I thought perhaps it might provide me something to do during these periods. Although I've been in the market from time to time, one of your sales people convinced me that I didn't have to know anything about the market to attend . . . and to benefit. Another customer service representative recommended that I come prepared to trade . . . to open a stock account, et cetera, so I did.*

You will note from my resume that I spent ten years as a university professor and about the same on the "seminar" and "consulting" circuit. I know from experience that only a few out of a seminar ever really benefit . . . not because the seminar isn't good, but because most tend not to apply what they learn. I didn't want to be one of those, so I took the tapes mailed with your "Financial Power Pack" and listened to them . . . and listened to them . . . and listened to them. Even during the class breaks, I continued to replay them, et cetera. They were helpful in that

I had an idea about what would be discussed during class and became familiar with some of the terminology.

I've always enjoyed a "good" seminar and this one was. I must admit I was skeptical, mostly because of the perceived "hype" that went with the "selling." However, the class did deliver on what it promised (a seminar that "works,"what a novel approach).

I opened an account with $5,000. If I made money (which I had reservations about), great. If I lost money then it wouldn't be "great" but it would occupy some of the time before I began directing again. I must admit, I didn't expect what followed.

I began trading on the first day and knew immediately that I'd opened an account with the wrong broker when he began to argue with me about my trade. What I didn't want to do was jump into his company "hot stock of the day." While I knew nothing about the market, I didn't just fall off the banana boat either. Fortunately, there was a broker attending the WSWS that understood what the class was doing and was able to produce buy/sell slips demonstrating that he was actually making the trades being discussed in class. I opened an account with him and the choice has turned out to be a very good one. There was no "training" of the broker required. In fact he was (and has been) very supportive of the "Cook-Concepts." (In fact, he'll be attending the Wealth Academy with me in June.)

I won't bore you with the class trading details but by Friday following Thursday's class end, my $5,000 had grown to nearly $15,900. That got my attention! I added another $15,000 to the account and a little over a month later, my account was nearing

$100,000. I added another sum of money and similar results have followed since then.

I wanted to learn each of the strategies taught, so I tried a number of them.

For example:
Sample Option Plays:

Bought Coke (KO) Options at $4.625 and sold after a split at $6.50

Bought Iomega (IOMG) Options at $6 and sold at $10.25

Bought Accustaff (ACST) Options at $3.25 and sold at $4.875

Sample Covered Calls:

QuaterDeck (QDEK) bought stock at $14 and sold options twice

Egghead (EGGS) stock at $12 and sold calls at $1.9375

Network Express (NETK) at $12, sold calls at $.875 and called out at $12.50

IMP Inc. (IMPX) stock at $17.50, sold calls at $.9375

Sample Rolling Stock:

Bought ScoreBoard (BSBL) at $4.125 and sold at $5.636 (dropped & bought again)

Network Express (NETK) at $3.23 and sold at $5

. . . and I could go on with some 23 other trades. I lost on five of them. Of the five, three of the losses were my fault, not the system. And listen, Mr. Cook, if you think driving a taxi doesn't qualify a person to be in the market, try movie directing. This

morning I bought 10 contracts of HBOC at $12 and now three
hours later I just sold the calls at $13.50. It's only a 12.5%
return, but annualized it's 4,562.5%. Not too shabby for a few
hours work.

As I said earlier, I'd had a successful career in the consulting
and seminar field so I always appreciate a good seminar (most
are not). And, as much as I like the Wall Street Workshop, I
would have paid the fee just for the last day's entities' seminar.
Aside from my market success, I will save enough in taxes from
that one day to pay not only for the Wall Street Workshop, but
for every other seminar that you offer, the courses you sell, the
books, manuals and chapters, WIN, et cetera.   And, you will
note from your sales records in my account that I've gotten about
everything you have (paid for by the WSWS course).

Since the course, I've read your new "hit" in detail, studied
the **Zero to Zillions** home study course, watched and re-
watched the WSWS Video Tape Sets, et cetera. Since the first
course was so good, I've signed up for the June "Wealth
Academy" and will be attending the "Next Step Wall Street
Workshop," et cetera. It's going to take a lot more than the 5
star entities to handle my business (I already have six), so I'll
also be at the "Executive Retreat." The best of all this is that I
haven't paid for a dime of it. The earnings have more than
covered everything.

I like your style so much that I've registered for the June
"Real Estate Boot Camp" but this time, I'm bringing my wife.
Now talk about someone without a background for real estate .
. . my wife, Deborah, is an actress (she had one of the leads in The
Winds of War and lead in Kotch with Walter Mathau, the lead

in Class of '44, *and the lead in* The Outing, *et cetera). But, she, like myself, has interests in things outside our field . . . particularly where they are profitable. To keep it in the family, my son will be attending your youth WSWS in August. It's a great idea. I would have liked to have had this background when I was his age.*

The concept of teaching the youth financial concepts when they are young is terrific. If I can help you in any way, please don't hesitate to ask.

Mr. Cook, thanks for being in the "business." The only problem is that now I'm enjoying the market more than the other things that I'm doing . . . a nice problem!

> *Best Regards,*
> *Dr. Warren C.*

Okay, let's say he only makes $250,000 on the initial $5,000. Let's say that's you. You're two days of training away from having the skills to do this. If it is you, and you are into safety, remember, you have your $95,000 worth of good, solid investments to make you feel good at night and when you get your portfolio's statements. Hopefully, the dividends and growth of the stocks will give you 10% plus per year. That could be $10,000 (of which only a small portion is cash). You've got the best of both worlds; aggressive cash flow <u>and</u> stability.

CONTENTS
FROM "STOCK MARKET MIRACLES"

Putting It All Together

12

*A*s I said earlier, information does not necessarily equal understanding. Knowledge of trading strategies, derivatives, and other alternatives in the market can cause more harm than good if they are not backed up with real discipline and an understanding of the basics. So, before enacting anything you have learned here or elsewhere, always consider the basics of investing. The strategies in this book are useless unless they are based on a sound, basic portfolio.

I outlined some guidelines in chapters one through three, and recommend that you read further in that area if you lack experience in the market. The financial language which includes price to earnings ratios, growth rates, debt ratios, dividend yields, asset allocation, and the myriad of other terms related to the market is important to have at least a passing familiarity with. Invest the time to learn about money before you invest your money.

There are several key points in this book that I believe are worth summarizing, in hopes that what you have read will make a real difference in your investing success. Some may seem obvious, but I find that even the most intelligent people I know make the same very human decisions when investing. Here are some points to remember.

Build a high quality portfolio. No amount of strategy, trading, or information can replace the basics of investing in high-quality, well-managed, future-oriented companies. Forget what you have just read until you have built your financial future on the basics. Get qualified professional help if you need to, but make sure the foundation of your portfolio is built on quality, not just on investments that look good in a bull market.

Plan for your future, and let your investments follow. Plan for what you will need to meet your goals, whether they are to retire i n comfort, send four children to college, or buy a new yacht. If through your planning you determine that you need to double your money every year, you need to invest more principal now or adjust your goals. Be realistic, and include the effects of taxes, inflation, and market fluctuations in your planning. I also recommend that most investors obtain the services of a professional. Find someone who is aware of investment alternatives, changes in tax laws, estate planning issues, and many other issues which may help you reach your goals sooner or with less risk.

Begin investing as early as possible. A 30 year old investor should have a very different portfolio that someone who is just about to retire. While much of this book is about controlling risk, don't let fear limit your long term returns. If you are young and have many years of earnings ahead of you, a more aggressive stance is completely appropriate. Conversely, if you are not able to replenish capital that could be lost in the market, you should choose investments with a very low likelihood of loss. Before investing anything, identify who you are as an investor and determine what kind of portfolio is right for you.

Proper asset allocation and diversification reduce risk. This book has hopefully provided some basic ideas as to the different types of assets classes, but you should put some serious thought into what is right for your portfolio. Remember to at least consider all types of assets in your thinking, such as international securities, hard assets/commodities, and real estate. Asset allocation will determine a large part of your portfolio's return over the long term. A widely quoted study done by Ibbotson Associates revealed the following:

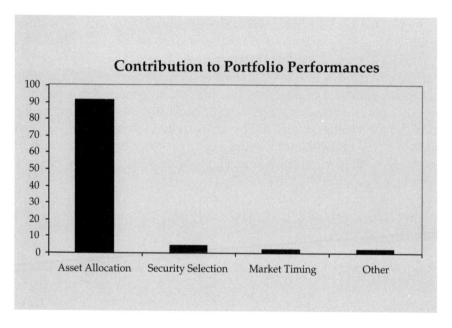

Contribution to Portfolio Performances

Though it is surprising to most people, asset allocation accounted for 91.5% of the performance (good or bad) in the portfolios studied. Maybe even more, since security selection (4.6%) is arguably a function of asset allocation. Allocation includes placing your assets in different asset classes (bonds, stocks, et cetera), styles (value vs. growth, for instance), and sectors (steel, semiconductors, publishing, et cetera). If the semiconductor sector is experiencing a tremendous rally, you will be experiencing gains with almost any stock in the sector. You will probably do best with the strongest companies in the sector, of course.

The other two factors are essentially negligible in their real effect. Over time, market timing (1.8%) has little effect, because I believe it is impossible to sell at the top and buy at the bottom with any sort of consistency. The "Other" (2.1%) category, which includes trading costs and management fees, can of course grow to a larger percentage when portfolios are turned over too frequently. The basic lesson is that a majority of your time should be spent allocating your assets, not worrying about the market or the smaller costs associated with enacting your portfolio management decisions.

Avoid losses. Remember how insurance works: identify risk, quantify it, then act to reduce its effect on your assets. *Identify, Quantify and Reduce.* Stocks, bonds, and most other investments fluctuate in price. This is a normal part of investing. If you cannot afford to take a loss but can rationally identify risk in an investment, either sell the investment or take other steps to mitigate the loss should it occur. Cut losing investments and let winning investments reach their full potential whenever possible. This is called a sell discipline. Understanding when to sell or hedge is just as important as knowing when and what to buy.

Time in the market is far more important than timing the market. Our natural tendency is to buy at the top and sell at the bottom. Truly successful investors are committed to remain in the market through its ups and downs. Though they may make adjustments in their asset allocation from time to time according to market conditions, they are never out of the market.

It is possible to make money in flat or declining markets. Staying in the market does not necessarily mean gritting your teeth and waiting for better days. It does mean remaining invested and taking steps to make sure your portfolio is properly positioned, and hedged if necessary, for your situation. There are usually at least some investments which are rising when the majority are falling. The opposite is also true—it is very possible to lose money in rising markets. Remember that an index is simply an average of many different investments. If the Dow Jones Industrial Average goes up, it does not mean that every one of the stocks in it rose. As I write this, the Dow Jones Industrial Average is up 20% and the NASDAQ Composite is up 22% year to date. However, 43% of all NASDAQ stocks and 27% of the stocks on the New York Stock Exchange are *down* from where they began the year. In 1994, the NASDAQ Composite fell 3% for the year, yet over 40% of the stocks within it showed a gain for the year! Try to include investments and strategies in your portfolio that will rise or maintain their value when the averages may be falling.

Portfolios managed for instant gratification frequently fail in the long term. Only your own progress towards your goals should matter, so ignore the noise in the market. Adjust your portfolio occasionally, using your investment plan and some basic investment criteria that you believe work for you. If an investment no longer meets the criteria which caused you to buy it, then get rid of it. This may happen frequently, as change is rapid in today's economy and the market. However, make sure you are trading on real fundamentals, not short term fluctuations.

Have the resources you need for success. Today's investor has more information available than ever before. The unprecedented bull market of the past few years has combined with the advent of the internet to make many things available that never have been before. Never has so much been available in the way of raw data. It pays to learn to use these resources because you can never be too informed. However, though I am admittedly biased in saying so, I believe that most investors benefit in using the services of a professional investment advisor as well. There are exceptions to this, such as when the investor is willing to commit to learning all of the things necessary to actually be their own advisor. Since much of what experienced financial consultants know comes through actual gains and losses, the education can be expensive when you are running your own portfolio.

My own bias is towards investment advisors who work on a flat fee basis (no trading commissions or other charges). The charges should generally be between .50 and 2.5% of a portfolio, depending on services required and portfolio size. Fee based management aligns the interests of the broker and the client, so both make more or less money according to the portfolio's performance over time. I also recommend utilizing a financial consultant with one of the larger investment

31

banks. Despite the many changes on Wall Street in the past decade, it is my opinion that these large players are still the primary source of research, new offerings, product inventory, and consistent trading execution for their clients. Hire someone who you trust to offer advice, information, and insight as a part of your financial team, not just a broker to execute trades. Keep in mind that my background and my future are at such a firm, so I am naturally biased. That is for these very reasons. My clients are best served with the capabilities of a true investment bank, not just a place where I can execute trades. Your portfolio is as good as the person who is helping you manage it, so take as much care in selecting your advisor as you would in choosing a doctor. Both professionals will (or should) know everything about your health, whether physical or financial. Like your doctor, your financial advisor should be someone who you trust to make informed decisions which are in your best interest.

During years of restless sleep filled with nightmares of what the market would hand me on the following day, I began to envy my children as they slept. They were oblivious to the financial world that obsessed my thoughts, and were dreaming peacefully while I paced the halls of our home in fits of insomnia. Then, I began to learn that worry need not be a part of investing when you have the proper perspective and information.

Armed with some basics and the strategies in this book, I hope you will be able to invest in the market with a higher degree of comfort than the average investor. The keys to success are discipline and perspective. Ignore the noise that is ever present in the market, keep your eye on the long term, and manage your portfolio in an objective manner. Concentrate on informed opinion and facts. Carefully build your own plan to reach your goals. Your ability to grow and use your assets in the future is all that really matters in the final analysis.

Contents

from "Sleeping Like A Baby"

Use your commute time to enhance your financial security. Call **1-888-ASK-WADE** today and order the "Zero-to-Zillions" audio series.

Chapter 8

Bear Traps

*When you reach for the stars,
you may not get one,
but you won't come up with a
handful of mud either.*
—Leo Burnett

Follow these ten steps and you are guaranteed to fail in the stock market. True poverty and frustration will be yours.

1. Don't diversify. Keep all your eggs in one basket. Keep life simple. Bet it all on red. Also, don't learn functional methods to increase your cash flow. Variety is not the spice of life. Anyway, you don't need more income, so stick with the "buy one stock and hang on" theory.

2. Don't read anything. There's so much weird stuff in the world, so what's the use? Don't seek out a diversity of opinions. There's too much information available—our minds are on information overload already. So, don't explore. Don't be concerned with the economic "signs of the times."

Excerpt from "Bear Market Baloney"

3. Look at past performance of stocks and invest in companies affected poorly by a recession or by negative conditions. Look for the worst, buy into the worst, be the worst.

4. Don't worry about income. You won't need more cash flow later so don't sell anything—including options (to generate income) on stocks you already own.

5. Don't worry about the quality of your stockbroker. Anyone will do. If they say or do negative things, follow them. If they bad mouth education, seminars, books, then follow their advice. If they want to be your only link to the world of profits, then go for it. If they're not "up" on it, they'll be "down" on it. (Note: The author believes a good stockbroker can make you a fortune, but you've got to find and train him/her to be good). And don't think of having two stockbrokers. Who would want a second opinion, or someone else finding good deals?

6. Make sure you ask the opinion of everyone at work and church—especially those making $35,000 or less a year. They're tuned in to what's going on. Also, seek out people who know someone who lost their shirt in _____ (gold, stocks, business, real estate). You fill in the blank. Avoid successful people.

7. Pay no attention to fundamentals (analysis). Ignore earnings—especially companies with increasing earnings. A company's debt is of no concern, so don't worry about it. Who cares about dividends and yields?

Beware of inside information . . . all inside information.
—Jesse Livermore

8. Play every insider tip you have. News from people "in the know" is very hard to come by. Shoot the wad on it. Who cares what they (whoever leaked the news, or made it up) have to gain by it.

9. Ignore temporary dips, or pull back. Remember, opportunity only knocks once. For you, it was when you were 23, so why look for more chances to make money now?

10. Don't educate yourself. It's a waste. Avoid the Wall Street Workshop at all costs. Who wants to learn how to double your money every two and a half to four months? Who wants to be retired in ten months? And anyway, who wants to be in a 40% tax bracket? Stay home and stay poor—let's not upset

In a bear market,
what's the difference between a stockbroker
and a pigeon?
The pigeon can still make a deposit
on a BMW!

the apple cart. Whoever said, "You pay for education once, you continually pay for ignorance," just didn't know what they were talking about.

To get anything you want, you have to take a risk at
some point and say "Yes!" Say "Yes!" to your financial
dreams today by calling **1-800-872-7411**.
Ask about Wade's "180 Degree Cash Flow Turnaround"
video for the answers you need.

Contents
from "Bear Market Baloney"

The man looked into the rationale behind this theory to see if the stock market was truly played out. Instead, he found that the fundamental driving forces for a bull market are still in place. The fear of a downtrend was unfounded. He even found reasons to expect that the current upward trend could continue for several years into the next century. He relaxed, and he began to focus again on teaching people how to take advantage of this rising tide. The principal that made these formulas work was called the Money Machine. But it didn't start with the stock market...

(Continued on page 51)

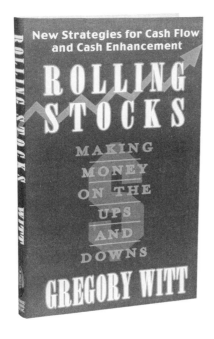

2

ROLLING TO RICHES

If you are like most investors you probably started out in the stock market by buying a stock with the intent of holding on to it for a long time. As you gained experience and confidence in your investing ability, you realized that by buying on dips and selling on strength, you could generate greater returns.

The Rolling Stock strategy takes that basic principle and multiplies it repeatedly. By focusing on repeated, short-term gains, there is a cumulative and compounded return that you won't find with a "buy and hold" strategy. The Rolling Stock strategy increases the emphasis on the selling of stock. The fact is, if you are like most investors, you don't spend a lot of time thinking about selling stock.

If you are like most investors I talk with, you will be able to quickly understand and apply the Rolling Stock strategy. In fact, I've never taught this strategy and then had someone say "I don't get it," or "Please explain that again; I didn't understand what you were doing." Rolling Stock is such a simple, powerful strategy that it's never misunderstood.

My challenge is to help investors recognize how really effective a Rolling Stock strategy can be in generating cash quickly and in transforming a small account into a large account in a short time frame.

Fortunately there are plenty of great examples to illustrate the power of Rolling Stocks. If you doubt the effectiveness of Rolling

"The greatest accomplishment is not in never falling, but in rising again after you fall."

—VINCE LOMBARDI

Stocks or if you think there just isn't enough to be gained by buying on dips, let's see what we can learn from this example.

JUST An Example

To demonstrate the power of Rolling Stocks, let me show you a straightforward, real life example of the kind of phenomenal returns Rolling Stocks can generate. The name of the company we'll use for our example is Just Toys Inc. (Ticker JUST).

For illustrative purposes, I am not going to mention commissions in this example. Commissions are a real cost of trading, as are capital gains taxes. You should never fail to take the cost of commissions into account as you determine your entrance and exit point. I'll talk about managing commissions in Chapters 6 and 11, but let's learn the fundamental strategy first.

In this example I am going to put all numbers in dollars and cents rather than fractions. This will make it easier to follow and relate our holdings to our real life pocketbook. Thus, $2^{13}/32$ becomes $2.41. Not only does it make sense to more people, but it also represents the current trend, as several markets have chosen to convert to decimals in 1998.

Just Toys Inc. designs, develops, manufactures, and markets toys, sports equipment, and games. Their stock trades on the NASDAQ under the ticker JUST. They make AirZone sports toys and polyvinyl chloride bendable figures known as Bend-Ems. Most of these toys are based on characters from Disney, Warner, and 20th Century Fox cartoons. The company sells to mass merchandisers such as Wal-Mart, K-Mart, Target, and Toys R Us.

The stock traded as high as $23 in 1993 and made a steady decline through most of 1994 on disappointing earnings. By 1995 the stock was trading in a more stable pattern under $3 a share. As you can see this is no Intel; it's not even a Mattel!

To make spectacular returns in Rolling Stocks you don't need to find a high-flying growth company. Let's take a look at how a repeated roll can turn a small fortune into a much larger fortune in a short period of time.

"If you think you can, you can. If you think you can't, you're right."

—Mary Kay Ash

Roll #1. During May and early June, 1995, Just Toys (JUST) established support at $1.25 per share. It traded as low as $1, but it would have been easy on any of several days to buy it at $1.25 or less. For the sake of this example, let's be conservative and say that you purchased 1,000 shares for $1.25 or a total investment of $1,250.

At this point, the first rule of Rolling Stock comes into play: "Know when to get out." That is, determine where and when you will sell. By looking at the chart, we can determine that the previous support level of $2 would be a likely new resistance level. So we then put in a Good Till Canceled (GTC) order to sell at $2.

Within three weeks the stock was trading around $2 per share. It even went as high as $2.44 on one day, and traded for several days at $2.25 or higher. Now the second rule comes into play: "Don't be greedy." We don't have to catch the absolute top and bottom of the range to make phenomenal returns. All the technical indicators were saying "sell, sell, sell." Some of these technical indicators include volume, stochastics, moving averages and other factors. Our GTC did its job and we were filled at $2. Our initial investment of $1,250 has now grown to $2,000 in just a few short weeks.

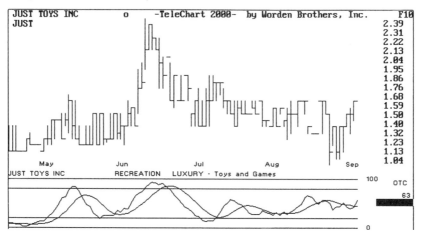

	Buy	Price of Stock	Shares	Cost	Price of Stock	Sell	Proceeds
Roll 1	6-95	$1.25	1,000	$1,250	$2	6-95	$2,000

"Nine-tenths of wisdom consists in being wise in time."

—THEODORE ROOSEVELT

43

Roll #2. By late August, JUST was trading back in the $1.25 range. It traded in this range for a full week. During that time you could have bought for as low as $1. Let's stay on the conservative side and put our buy order in for $1.25

In no less than four days the price of the stock shot up to our exit price of $2 per share. If your GTC was in place your stock would have sold. Over the next month the stock traded around and above the $2 range. It even went as high as $2.63 in both September and October.

Roll #3. By December, JUST had slowly declined back down to a decent buy range. You could have bought it at or below $1.25 for over a week. But the best technical indicators had us buying it on December 27th.

Patience is a good virtue to have in the stock market, because you had to wait 49 trading days before the stock hit $2. Again, you would have been filled on February 28, 1996 at $2 but only if your had your GTC in place.

Roll #4. It took only 19 trading days in March for JUST to slide back down to the $1.25 buy range. The stock drops as low as $1.13, but we wait for the optimal technical buy signals and purchased it at $1.25. Needless to say, we put in a GTC to sell at $2

Thank goodness the GTC was in place. Within two days the stock jumped to $2 and we got out. We then move on to other opportunities while the stock moves down to our buy range.

"All progress has resulted from people who take unpopular positions."

—ADLAI STEVENSON

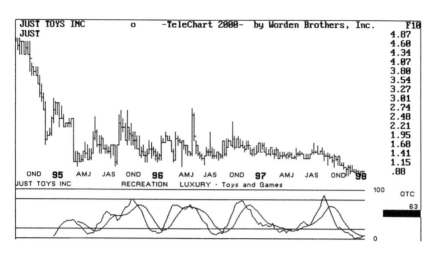

	Buy	**Price of Stock**	**Shares**	**Cost**	**Price of Stock**	**Sell**	**Proceeds**
Roll 1	6-95	$1.25	1,000	$1,250	$2	6-95	$2,000
Roll 2	8-95	$1.25	1,600	$2,000	$2	8-95	$3,200
Roll 3	12-95	$1.25	2,560	$3,200	$2	2-96	$5,120
Roll 4	4-96	$1.25	4,096	$5,120	$2	4-96	$8,192

Roll #5. This buying opportunity occurs in just 17 trading days as we saw the stock go as low as $1. But again, let's be conservative and make our entrance at $1.25 on April 29, 1996. We put in our GTC then hold our shares and wait 24 trading days and watch our stock be sold for $2 a share on June 3rd.

Roll #6. Greed tempts us and we almost start to kick ourselves as the stock goes up to a high of $2.69. But that sour grapes feeling is short lived as JUST makes its predictable slide back down to the $1.25 range in 18 days.

During August, 1996, the stock traded at or below $1.25 for three weeks. During this time the stock goes as low as $1.06. We watch the technical indicators and buy at the end of the trough at $1.25.

We make our smooth entrance and put in our GTC to sell at $2 a share. Within 14 trading days the stock hits $2 and we are out on August 5, 1996. This time its retreat is more precipitous and falls back to the buy range in just seven days.

"Success is never final."

—WINSTON CHURCHILL

45

Roll #7. JUST stays in the $1.25 buy range for over a month. The technical indicators are particularly weak. We could get in at any time for $1.25, but if we wait for the strongest signals, we buy back in on September 17th.

In just 24 trading days our prized possession made its familiar climb back up to $2. Our GTC to sell is doing its job and we are filled on October 21st.

Following the seventh roll and the sale of the stock, JUST flattened out in a narrower range. It stayed in that range for over a year. Finally, in November, 1997, JUST fell down into the $1.25 range. The technical indicators were particularly weak, and I saw no compelling buy opportunity.

The stock continued to fall below the $1 level at the time of this writing. Technical indicators remain weak, but I continue to monitor both the fundamentals of the company and the technical indicators on the stock price.

As you can see, by applying the Rolling Stocks strategy and using the techniques which detail in the following chapters you could have rolled JUST seven times in 17 months. But the most exciting part is what happened to your trading capital in each successive roll.

Assuming you reinvested your initial trading capital and continued using the proceeds of each sale to buy more shares, your initial investment of $1,250 to buy 1,000 shares would have grown to 16,777 shares which would have generated cash proceeds in your account of $33,553. That's a 2,584% rate of return in just 17 months!

	Buy	Price of Stock	Shares	Cost	Price of Stock	Sell	Proceeds
Roll 1	6-95	$1.25	1,000	$1,250	$2	6-95	$2,000
Roll 2	8-95	$1.25	1,600	$2,000	$2	8-95	$3,200
Roll 3	12-95	$1.25	2,560	$3,200	$2	2-96	$5,120
Roll 4	4-96	$1.25	4,096	$5,120	$2	4-96	$8,192
Roll 5	4-96	$1.25	6,553	$8,192	$2	6-96	$13,107
Roll 6	7-96	$1.25	10,485	$13,107	$2	8-96	$20,971
Roll 7	9-96	$1.25	16,777	$20,971	$2	10-96	$33,553

"We know what a person thinks not when he tells us what he thinks, but by his actions."

—ISAAC BASHEVIS SINGER

Also, in the above example, your money wasn't even invested most of the time. While you were waiting for JUST to make its descent back to the $1.25 buy range, you could have taken the proceeds and invested those in another Rolling Stock.

Maybe it's not realistic to expect that the average investor could have caught all seven rolls. But even if you caught only four or five of the rolls, you would have walked away with a 555% rate of return in less than a year. Is that better than what you're currently getting?

Now you decide. Are you ready to learn the Rolling Stock strategy? Are you ready to turn your stock market account into a cash flow locomotive? Do these kinds of returns on publicly traded companies interest you? Then let's keep rolling!

"I had no ambition to make a fortune. Mere money-making has never been my god. I had an ambition to build."
—JOHN D. ROCKEFELLER

Contents
from "Rolling Stocks"

Rolling Stocks is one of four powerful stock strategies taught at Wade Cook Seminars' Financial Clinics.
Call **1-800-872-7411** to set a date and sign up for a financial clinic in your area.

SECTION 2

How the Dream Began

Many years before he was successful teaching about the stock market, this young man wanted to teach college. He needed income to pay for his schooling, so he began an insurance agency. He thought he could sell enough policies to create ongoing income from premiums, but even though he worked hard and became successful, it was difficult making enough money to support his family and go to college.

He resolved to find a way to produce more income through other means. First, he borrowed a little money and bought his first rental house. Second, he got a job on the side driving a taxicab. That first day on the streets of Tacoma, he learned something that would change his life forever—something he called the Meter Drop.

Anyone who's ever ridden a taxi knows that as soon as you get in, the meter starts out automatically with $1.50 to $2.00 toward the fare. It didn't take long for the young cabbie to figure out that it was easier and faster to make money by doing a lot of small, short-term runs than by waiting around for one big run. So, instead of holding out for the long, "big-ticket" rides to the airport, he drove around town picking up many short fares often ignored by other cabbies, making money on every run.

The young man put the Meter Drop principle to work in his cab driving right away, but it took a crisis for him to begin to see the larger implications of the Meter Drop. While he was working at his insurance agency and driving the cab, the man had also continued to buy, fix up, and rent small properties. His asset base grew steadily, and soon he was considered pretty well off for the economy and his age—at least on paper. In reality, though, he was cash-flow poor, struggling to meet his monthly bills even as his net worth grew. There finally came a time when he was unable to pay a $60 electric bill. To come up with the money, he decided to sell one of his properties.

Many people told him not to do this, that he would regret it. The conventional wisdom on income real estate is to buy and hold on for all you are worth. Our young man was not so conventional, however. He went against all the advice he'd been given and sold a small rental house, and he even did this unconventionally, using owner financing. Basically, he acted as a bank or loan company for the buyer rather than getting all his cash out up front.

(Continued on page 63)

AN OVERVIEW OF THE MONEY MACHINE CONCEPT

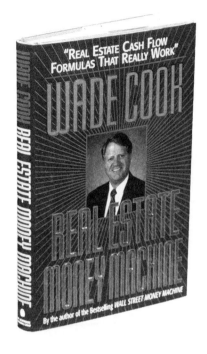

Awhile ago when I was writing my book *Real Estate for Real People*, I wanted to include a chapter on the Money Machine Concept. I wrote an extensive chapter. It said what I wanted it to, so now I am going to put that concept here to help you see the plan before you get into the specifics.

These past few years have been very enlightening. I've had the opportunity to be on several hundred radio and TV talk shows. At almost every one, the host has commented on my first book's first title: *How to Build a Real Estate Money Machine.* The most frequent remark is that it sounds like a get-rich-quick formula. My usual comeback is that it's just the opposite. I tell the host that when I was writing the book, the publisher said, "Look, Wade, we've got a hundred books on how to make a million dollars, can you write a book on how to make a living?"

It took a long time to come up with that title. Even though only a few people have said it correctly when introducing me, every word does have its place. Money doesn't grow on trees, and it doesn't come from a machine. The concept, though, is to build an investment portfolio that continually gives off a monthly income with very little start-up capital.

It's fun to share this concept here in brief form. The book has done very well, and letters come in from everywhere, proving that a single concept repeated often enough will bring success. Once you've read this concept, you'll realize two things: (1) It is true what the president of one company said: "I'd rather lose money and know how I lost it, than make money and not know how I made it." If we can do something repetitiously, we can become good at it, refine it, analyze it, and retire on it. It's not that the job becomes easier, it's that our ability to do it becomes better. (2) This is no get-rich-quick scheme. It takes many long hours of learning and doing. There are many "no's" on our way to the "yes," but it is attainable, and it sure beats the alternatives.

That last sentence is a good diving board to get us into the pool. For a long time, there were two philosophies for investing in real estate. One philosophy was to buy a property, fix it up, and then find someone to get a new loan and pay you off. You then took the money and did it again, only this time with a larger property. You kept repeating this process. It still works today on certain properties if they are purchased right. But the banks are too much in control, and it's almost impossible to stay on track, because the investor is not in control of most of the process.

The other philosophy is to buy and hold onto the property one day short of forever. Seminars teaching this method abound. This plan is also good if you buy low and get low payments, but it has two major drawbacks. The first drawback is that it usually takes cash for the down payment and closing costs. Most people have enough to buy only one property. Then they have to save up or borrow to get a second down payment. The second drawback is becoming a landlord and having all the attendant problems. I've been there. It's hard to get started and find that all you ever do is make repairs. In today's marketplace, there's so little profit (with the higher-than-usual monthly payments and rents that haven't kept up) that it seems as if landlords end up working for minimum wage.

The last thing I'll write about these two philosophies is that they just take too darn long. Most people get frustrated and give up. While the Money Machine Concept is not a get-rich-quick scheme, it sure isn't a get-rich-slow scheme either. It is a sensible, proven way to make good money because it solves the need for a steady monthly income. Hard work is needed to build it, but then the money just keeps rolling in.

I'll spend the next several pages explaining the process and telling you what a few others are doing. But first it would be helpful to explain the concept in a few sentences. Test me as you read the pages after the next paragraph and see if I deviate. Everything is part of a puzzle. We can't go on to C until we've done B. Remember, repetition is the key.

The Money Machine Concept is a system of *buying* good properties under market value with assumable loans, and hopefully, sellers who will take their equity (or most of it) in monthly payments. Then the properties are *fixed up* cosmetically and *resold* with you, the investor, getting back the money put in and taking *monthly payments* for the newly created equity, unless you have the option to get cashed out of the property, then take the cash! You have created a lien on each property, and that is your security. The new buyer does not assume the existing loans. He pays me his monthly payment, and I turn around and pay the previous owner my monthly payment. This is called a "wraparound."

If that sounds like a mouthful, it is. But, like any concept, once it is explained and understood, you will say, "Aha!" It's like learning the secret to a magic trick.

Buying

We have to buy right. The word "right" used here means that the terms and conditions of buying have to be conducive to selling. People often ask, "What if I can't sell it?" I truthfully reply, "Don't buy it." Only buy that which you can resell quickly. A good house in a fair to good neighborhood is the right choice. Buy in lower-middle-income neighborhoods. If you see people jogging, leave; those are the wrong neighborhoods. Blue collar workers don't come home and go jogging. Blue collar neighborhoods are the right neighborhoods to invest in because they are where most people live. One other point: people getting rich and people getting poor have to live in the neighborhoods. We'll get them coming and going.

Buy houses with assumable loans. You're not going to hide anything from banks, so if they are going to be a problem, don't buy that house. Look for loans with an interest rate under 12%. FHA and VA loans are fully assumable. It costs a small name-change fee. There is no qualifying by you or anyone who may own the property in the future. We're obviously looking for diamonds in the rough. The old adage about buying the worst house in the best neighborhood is good advice.

Constantly be looking and have others looking for you. Carry a purchase agreement in the glove compartment, because good deals are everywhere. Keep in mind that, at first, finding these good deals seems like the hardest thing to do, but after a few weeks or a few months on the streets, this will be the easiest part.

For a moment, let's talk about monthly payments. The hard part is to find people who are willing to take monthly payments for their equity. Most people want cash. We need to get to people before they've mentally spent their money, so we can educate them on the beauty of monthly payments. I love monthly payments and would rather have $100 a month for 22 years than $10,000 cash, especially when I create the $100 from virtually nothing. If you think you'll have a hard time explaining to people why they should take monthly payments from you instead of a lump sum, you can show them a pamphlet I've written that explains all the reasons why monthly payments are beneficial. It's called *Owner Financing*, and because it's only 50 pages, it will be convenient for prospective sellers to read. (For your copy, call Lighthouse Publishing Group, Inc. at 1-800-706-8657.)

Back to the buying process. The main thing to remember when buying is to guard your cash. When you sell, it has to be a good deal for the next person, and if you're demanding too much down, you won't find a buyer. When I buy, my average down payment is 4% of the purchase price, and when I sell, the average down payment I receive is 6% of the new selling price.

While "down payments in" and "down payments out" are important, the whole buying process bogs down if the monthly payments are out of line. When average people buy a property, they have to think about many things: the purchase price, the down payment, the monthly payments, the interest rate, and so on. Of these concerns, the monthly payment required either makes or breaks the deal. If this aspect is so important to the next person who will buy the house (or rent it for that matter), should it not be our number one consideration when we are buying? This is called "second-generation thinking." Most of us get bogged down thinking first generation. We just think how we like the house, how the monthly payment affects us, and how we respond to the neighborhood. Most problems in real estate investing wouldn't occur if the investor would think about the next buyer—the second generation.

Handle the purchase by the book. Use competent professionals to take care of details such as drawing up the papers, and obtaining title insurance.

Fix-Up

The main idea, once again, is to guard your cash. If some people want to fix up a house to be fit for a king, let them. Instead, you should just do light, cosmetic work and general cleanup. The fixing up you do should be to enhance and sell the already good deal that you've purchased. Here are five general pointers that will prove the point. Others will occur to you when you get in the middle of a project and ask yourself the question: "What else could I be doing with my time and money?"

1. Fix up your houses for women. Women buy real estate. The final decision is theirs. I'm reminded of a story about a man up in heaven. There were two doors. One door was marked "For Henpecked Husbands," and there was a long line of men standing in front of it. The other door was marked "For Men Who Are The Boss," and there was only one man standing in front of that door. When asked why he was standing there, he replied: "I don't know. My wife told me to." Women control the purchase of real estate.

2. Use one color of paint in all your houses and apartments. A nice, off-white is best. It goes with everything and makes small rooms look larger. Using one color will also save money because it can be bought in large quantities. Also, you won't have a rainbow of leftover paint cans cluttering up your garage.

3. Don't dicker with your subcontractors on the price of fixing up. If you compromise on the amount of money you'll pay them, the quality of their work will go down.

4. Commit people working on your houses to an ending time for their work. If you don't, the job won't get done on time and guess who gets stuck with making payments on a vacant house?

5. Buy wholesale. You don't need a license. Just tell hardware, plumbing, and electrical stores that you're remodeling many houses and want to set up an account.

Selling

So far, there has been a method to your madness. Everything makes sense, and now that the property is livable, you sell it. The terms of selling have to be a good deal for the next person. Many people are renting today because they can't afford the monthly payments. If people can rent a $100,000 house for $800 a month, why should they purchase it for $1,000 plus per month?

Every detail has to be fair. The down payment you charge has to be under 10% of the new selling price. You can charge more, but you'll probably have to wait. The interest rate should be under 12%, if possible, so the payment can stay affordable. The price should also be slightly under market value, so some profit is left for the next person. You buy low and sell just below high.

No one has ever written a book on *selling* real estate. I don't know why. In every other business, profits are made when something is sold. Granted, there are many advantages to holding real estate, but the selling aspect is so often overlooked. I contend that the way to faster profits is to treat the investments like a business.

I produced a seminar book and course entitled *Sell Your Own Property*. In it are hundreds of tips on selling: when to sell, when not to, how to structure the transaction, and others. But nothing works in the book and nothing works in life unless the selling of the property is a good deal for the next person. This concept is not complicated. Your horse sense will get you over the hurdles. Map out a plan and minimize the obstacles.

Why go through all this trouble? Because when it's time to sell, you want to have all of your doors open. You want to be able to sell the property in any way you please. If you've taken on a loan with a due-on-sale clause, many doors slam closed. If you put in too much money, the door of selling with very little down on a wraparound or assumption closes. Keeping all of your doors open takes cautious planning.

Also, make sure all the terms and conditions of buying are conducive to selling. It doesn't take much to figure out that being cautious in buying the property and taking care to ascertain all future possibilities will force you to make a good deal. Just think of the alternatives—if you don't do this kind of planning and structuring, the results can be horrendous. Most of the problems I have experienced, or now hear about, have their origin in the financing arrangements for purchasing the property. If this is the case, then be careful. All of your efforts for good leverage and tax write offs can go out the window with just one clause that restricts your right to sell. Be prepared to walk away from a bad deal that does this.

You don't want to create new problems by selling; you want to solve problems. Your first step is to see how selling will affect our other investments, especially your tax situation. It's amazing how fast selling one property affects the amount of taxes you would have to claim if you sold another one. You can go marching up through the tax brackets pretty quickly.

Real estate is so fun because you are not limited to just one way of selling; you can use different methods to solve different problems. You could hit a single (an installment sale for the entire amount, for example) and advance a little with very few tax implications, but with great monthly income. You could hit a double by getting some money down and carrying the balance. You could even hit a homer and get all of our money.

Perhaps you should wait for a while. The property might be a good rental unit, but the time to hit isn't right. You could even send in our designated hitter: switch the property for something else on a tax-deferred exchange. And it could be that after a few successful deals, you could take your mitt and ball and play a different game. I'm not recommending this—I'm just bringing up the possibility.

It's important and comforting to know that these selling methods are available. I suppose different ways have been developed with different tax savings, because so many people own and use real estate for their income, growth, and tax purposes. So let's explore some of the aspects of these ideas.

Cashing Out

Sometimes cashing out is the most preferred method, especially if there is a lot of money tied up or there are huge equities. You can accomplish this by having your buyer get new bank financing. You can help out by quickly getting the information the bank needs, or you could possibly lend the buyer the down payment by taking back a second or third mortgage.

Cashing out has an effect on your tax bracket, so you should watch this. Make sure other strategies (for instance, holding properties as rentals) are in place. If not, you may have to pay some taxes. Remember, if you anticipate tax consequences, set aside the applicable portion so the money is there when the taxes are due.

These questions always come up: what else could you be doing with the money? Are you willing to play the game with the IRS or the banks to get the property sold? Will you benefit more with the excess cash? Do you have other properties that you can get into? Are they lined up and ready to go?

Cashing out is one of the greatest enhancers to any investment plan. From all of my experience, though, I have found that he who relies solely on cashing out hoes a long row. It's nice, but there are other alternatives. What I'm suggesting here is this: don't go chasing after cash, but if cash comes chasing after you, take it.

For more information on how you can build a Real Estate Money Machine of your own, call: **1-888-862-8760** and ask about the *Live Real Estate Bootcamp!*

CONTENTS from "Real Estate Money Machine"

After receiving some money for the down payment, he came to realize something as he sat in his cab looking at the check. He had purchased a property with about $1,200 down, and even after closing costs he still had approximately $1,000 pure profit from selling. What was even better, from this small, quick deal he would be receiving net monthly payments of $125 from the buyer for the next 28 years.

All of a sudden, the Meter Drop principle and his original desire for continuing income came together, and the Money Machine concept was born...

Well, the young man was tremendously excited, and immediately went to work building his own Real Estate Money Machine. He focused on the Meter Drop, getting the property, selling the property, and getting on to the next deal. He was so successful he was able to retire and live off his Money Machine at the age of twenty-nine.

But after a few years of traveling and playing golf, he felt it was time to contribute more to his community. He decided to go back to his dream of teaching. He went to college, but discovered that many people wanted to know what he had done to be able to retire at such a young age. Rather than learn to teach

(Continued on page 93)

LEVERAGING PEOPLE

One of the greatest advantages of investing in real estate is that there is so much good material written on the subject and so many good lecturers traveling the country to share their knowledge. I want to pose this advantage for your consideration because if you understand the reason behind this educational drive, you'll be able to use their knowledge to great benefit.

Obviously, there is not enough time or money to allow you to make all the mistakes mentioned in this book. Other people have preceded you who are more than willing to share their experiences with you, but this idea goes further than that. Wouldn't it be great if you could pick and choose what information you need to get into and out of deals, deals you've never thought possible? After all, why should you reinvent the wheel?

The investment methods of the different states are more similar than they are different. If a woman in Texas solved a problem that is similar to one that you're having, then why not study her method? Perhaps you'll use it all, or perhaps you'll only use part of it—or even improve on it.

One big advantage of having these experts available is that they are content to sell their books or charge a fee for their seminar and consulting—and that's it. You can take their ideas and put them to work in your area, and anything you make is your own.

Many times I've wished that I could get a commission on the growth and income others have created from reading my books and attending my seminars. I don't say this to brag (though a little of that is not bad because I'm proud of what my staff and I have done), but only to prove a point. There is no way to keep track of how much has been made with the Money Machine concept and the ideas from my other books.

I love it! It makes me feel good to have so many people taking charge of their lives and doing so much with so little. I don't really want a commission on any of it. People have worked for it, and now they can enjoy the fruits of their labors.

People ask me why I keep up this pace. This book is as good a forum as any to explain this. If you can understand my motives, then perhaps you will understand the motives of my fellow speakers, and this will motivate you to educate yourself further.

I've made a lot of money investing in real estate. I invested in real estate so that I could teach. I've worked toward that since I was seventeen years old. I wanted to go back to college and had to create an income source to do that. I turned to real estate to accomplish this.

About the time I was to start back to school, I was asked to write a book. *Real Estate Money Machine* was the result, and with that I was off on the lecture circuit. I now teach more than I ever could in college, and I teach people who really want to learn.

Their successes drive me on. I really enjoy taking people from a point of not understanding something to a point of understanding something and, additionally, to a point where they actually take the information and put it to work for themselves. I have dedicated my career to this end. All of my books and seminars have several constant themes: stay out of trouble, avoid clutter, create cash flow, and take control of all aspects of your investments.

Well, enough about me. What about the other authors and lecturers? I would say that very few of them are in it for the money. If that were the case, we'd follow our own investment advice and make more money by actually investing. Most are in it for the same reasons I mentioned. Most are good, honest people. You'll know when you hear them or when you read their books how much experience they've had and what kind of people they are.

I caution you, though, to beware. Test what they say for yourself. The story of the three little pigs is probably the best investment lesson ever taught. While two pigs were building their houses of straw and sticks, the third was building his house with bricks—one brick at a time. When the hard times came and the two other houses were lying on the ground, the brick house stood firm. Shouldn't our investment plan, our empire, be built the same way—one brick at a time?

Before I move on and explain how this can work for you, let me add one other thing. Most of these authors are extremely proud of their books, tapes, and other educational materials. Yes, there is a lot of outdated and irrelevant material out there, but there is also a lot of material with a great deal of thought and experience behind it. Look at how much pride they take in their books and seminars. The lecture circuit is a hard business. Very few make it. The only ones who do are honest and forthright and teach only good, functional information.

The Meaning for You

I'm sure that as you've read this you've thought of the books you've purchased and the money you've spent on seminars. Some of you might be thinking of gaining more education. Great! That's the way it should be. You'll open new doors, close a few bad ones, and polish the knobs on others.

It's a big investment world out there. We should stay educated. There is no standing still; the market isn't standing still, so neither should we. We should stay a step ahead by knowing what our education will do for us.

Excerpt From "Real Estate For Real People"

We're not going to invest in everything, but of those ideas we want to put to use, we can gather the best advice possible. Even contrasting opinions can help us establish a good function.

There are books and seminars on many different subjects. I don't recommend them all, but I've read and studied most of them. It's hard for me not to put in an advertisement here. My company publishes and sells many of these books, and we sponsor many seminars. But I do have a list of books and seminars I think are a must for different aspects of investing. I have included this list at the back of this book for your information.

Investment Groups

For the past several years many of the speakers have sponsored local investment groups. Almost every major city has at least one group that meets monthly. These people get together and have guest speakers talk about ideas pertinent to their area. Many have created buying privileges with local merchants. Anyone investing should attend because it's good to meet other investors and let them help you stay motivated. Call your local Chamber of Commerce for information on the group in your city.

Your Team

There is one lesson that I've had to learn over and over again. I bring it up here so that some of you won't have to make the same mistake. It sounds so simple, and in theory it is. But in real life it's a hard concept to institute and to keep working. We cannot do everything ourselves. We need a team of professionals.

When the poet John Donne wrote, "No man is an island," he stated a truth that we need to understand. This game of investments is for real. It is hard but exciting work. However, all of the excitement disappears when we make too many mistakes or when it turns to drudgery.

The need for a professional team is compounded in today's society when the complexities of investing demand specialization. Yes, we may be moving toward becoming a specialist, as I mentioned, but, in the meantime, we can use others not only to help us over the rough spots but to actually create opportunities for us.

There's no sense having people around who stifle everything we do. We need support. But it would be just as detrimental to have people around who will not throw a bucket of cold water on us occasionally. There must be a balance between the two. It's hard to find that balance and to keep it. So much enters into the picture besides truth; all kinds of feelings and personal biases become involved. My only advice is to keep cool. Consider the source and know what the source has to gain (or lose) by giving such advice.

Later on in this chapter, I'll list several possible members of your prospective team. I'll even show you ways to work with them, but before I do, let me list three points that will help put things in perspective.

First, the importance of having a team needs no long argument. I think we all know we need one. It may seem difficult, though, to find one—and it is. But I don't think that the process of setting one up or keeping it running should be so difficult that it stops us from doing the right thing.

As a matter of fact, this whole affair can really work to our advantage. There are many people who need help. What good professionals can do for us far outweighs the cost. They can get us into and out of properties we've never thought possible.

What I'm suggesting is that we look for and exploit the good that can happen. To explain this, let me tell of an experience I had with a professional roofer. Most of you probably want me to talk about real estate agents, lawyers, and CPAs. We'll get to that, but this story is too good and too pertinent to pass up.

I used a lot of inexperienced people to work on my properties. I found them at church or through friends or wherever. One Saturday I wanted to get a roof on a rather large house. I had had some experience with roofs before, so I thought it would take eight people to do the job.

Just before the work began, a professional roofer came by looking for work. He was very persuasive about his abilities. I really like a good sales pitch, so I took him on. This was new to me. The man actually wanted twice what I was paying any of the other eight workers. This man was so bold that I thought I'd have some fun, so I created a race. He would take one side of the house and the other eight workers would take the other side. He saw what I was doing and even went one better. He asked for the larger side.

They started work about 9:00 AM and dug in because the race was on. I checked in throughout the day, and after lunch it became clear who was going to win. The professional did win, but not by much. He finished his side at 3:30 PM, and the other eight finished at 4:00 PM His shingle lines were much straighter, and the whole side looked better. I became a believer. I paid the eight workers their $320 (8 people x 8 hours x $5 per hour = $320), and I paid the professional his $75 ($7 \frac{1}{2}$ hours x $10 per hour) and threw in a $25 bonus so he'd come back and work for me again.

It doesn't take a mathematician to figure out which way was better. This episode taught me some valuable lessons. I am not suggesting that you don't use inexperienced people, only that you consider the alternatives. If I take on someone who needs training, I'll be patient, but if they don't move on quickly to becoming an expert, then it's time to reevaluate and get someone who doesn't need to be pampered.

I hope you will draw many lessons from this. The point I'm trying to make is that we can learn a lot from setting up our team. We can take this disadvantage and turn it into an advantage. It's how we look at it. Our attitude will affect a good or bad outcome.

Second, if your team is set up right, it will be with people who have a great deal of experience working with other people. Not all of their advice will be exactly right, but much of it will come from lessons they've learned from the mistakes of others.

I've mentioned that we can learn by listening to, watching, and reading about the mistakes of others. But now, learning from the mistakes of others through the eyes of our professionals adds a special dimension: we get commentary with advice.

Isn't it nice to see success and failure and understand the "why" behind it? This is trite, but it needs to be said: we can't make all of the mistakes ourselves. There's not enough time, energy, or money to make them all. These people have been around for a while. Call them anything you like, but you can lump them all together in one title called "professional problem solvers." The better they are with others, the better they will be with us.

Third, every one of us wants to be independent: independently wealthy and an independent thinker. We want to be self-made. Great! I don't want to take being self-made away from anybody. I do, however, want to help everyone achieve this by adding a thought or two about interdependence.

From the successful people I've known and read about, it seems that they knew where they stood with others. They also understood their relationship between things, events, and time. They became truly independent once they knew how to put these other forces to work for them.

The story has often been told of Henry Ford and his board of directors. Ford surrounded himself with the most talented, creative minds possible. When asked a question, he would turn to the members of his team and get their opinions. Once he had heard the various sides, he'd make a decision. This gave him the freedom to be himself. We all need that freedom. The better our team of professionals, the more independence we'll have.

CONTENTS
From "Real Estate For Real People"

The Time Line

Before we get into the step by step process of how to find and process foreclosed properties, it would be well to understand what has happened to such a property. Let us see what will happen to this property in the future, and find out where on that timeline we can step into the picture.

Let us go to the beginning and see some of the problems that people incur. We will not only talk about these to show the beginning of the foreclosure time line, but also to lead the investor to the people who are having problems with their properties.

Obviously, a person does not buy a house thinking that he is going to be foreclosed on. At the time that he buys the house, all the information that he has given to the bank, FHA or VA has been truthful. But if there is one thing that is constant in this life, it is that nothing is constant. Everything changes. Unexpected things pop up in peoples' lives that they are not prepared for, causing undue difficulties. A person might lose a job, get sick, or have a death in the family. Because of these things, the payments stop. Then the person is quickly forced into a foreclosure sale.

Whatever the cause, the person quits making payments on the house. However, I have never seen anybody quit making payments on a house, with a thought of losing it. They felt like it was a temporary solution. They all felt that something would happen; something would change and they would be able to pull some kind of magic money out of their sleeve, curing the loan, and solving the problems with their house.

Many people think of house payments as if they were rent payments and they pay their house payments as if they were merely tenants. This is especially true with new homeowners. When money gets tight, the first area many people cut back on is the house payment.

The bank or lender obviously becomes very upset. They start writing nice letters at the beginning of the problem; trying to be kind so that the people will keep their savings account deposits with their bank. Then, after a month or two or three, the bank sends a notice that they are going to turn this over to their legal office to handle the problem. In this letter will be a strict warning of the things which can happen. The worst case is that the house will be taken away.

If the homeowner tries to make a payment during this time, the bank might accept that payment and then proceed, suing the people anyway. Most likely they will send the payment back and demand full payment, realizing that if they receive anything they have jeopardized their position. (What they would be saying is that it is okay for the homeowner to make late payments.) All payments, including the cost now of filing and sending such letters, will have to be paid in order for the loan to be actively reinstated.

If not paid, an attorney or representative of the lending institution has the papers turned over to him. He will immediately send out letters stating that he has been hired by the bank or the lending institution to act in the bank's behalf. He will usually give several alternatives to the homeowner in this letter, i.e., if you will pay the back payments by a specific date, it will be such and such an amount, but if you wait and pay the back payments by a later date, (which may be a couple months later and right before the foreclosure sale) then the payments and the costs will be so much more.

The person that is representing the bank will be required by law to file some kind of legal public notice. This may be done in the legal journal for the whole country, or it may be done in the local newspaper at the beginning or end of the classified section. In most states, this ad will have to run up to five or six times and usually once a week for a specified time before the actual trustee's sale or sheriff's sale.

This notification or announcement will state all the parties involved, the type of loan, mortgage, deed of trust or whatever legal document that is being foreclosed on. It will state the date that the sale will take place. It will usually include the latest date by which the problem can be taken care of, which is usually called the cure date.

It will also include the common address and legal description of the property. If it does not include the address, it is a simple matter of going to a title company or the county courthouse and looking up the legal description and finding the common address. It will also include the name of the attorney or the representative handling the sale and his phone number.

Now that these ads are placed, time goes on, and the person is still not making the payments. In most cases, the person now understands that he is in trouble and will probably lose the house. He will usually move out of the house rather than be hassled by the banks and people knocking on his door trying to get him to make up the monthly payments.

Many of today's loans are not good ones to assume, because you will be assuming the same problems (huge monthly payments or high interest rates) which the original owners are having. But, with these types of loans, the banks are starting to realize that they do not want to take these properties back. They might seem gruff, but getting these properties back only creates new problems and their people sometimes work with these homeowners in any way that they can.

If a property passes the cure date, it now goes to a trustee sale. It has passed the cure date. In most states the only person who would be able to cure after the cure date is the actual homeowner. Now the trustee or the attorney for the trustee, the beneficiary of the deed of trust or the mortgage, or even the Sheriff will go to the county courthouse, the city building, or wherever the legal records are kept for the county, and will stand in view of the public and auction it off. They will say, "I, as attorney for _____, representing _____, am here to auction off to the highest bidder, the property located at:_____." He will then proceed to read the legal description of the property.

Excerpt from "How To Pick Up Foreclosures"

He will also state the amount of the loan, the mortgage balance, the interest that is due and owing, and the amount of the court costs and foreclosure costs up to that time. He will lump them together in one sum and then state the total that the trustee bids. He will ask for any other bids, and if there is nobody there, he will say, "Going once, going twice, trustee takes possession, gone." At that point in time, he will notify the Sheriff of these proceedings. The Sheriff will order a writ of possession and now the homeowner has lost his house.

If the homeowner does not leave the house, the Sheriff's department will go there with the truck that has the big star on the side and will proceed to evict the people from the house. They will then impound everything in the house, including the furniture, the food, and the garbage. It will cost the homeowner several hundred dollars to get his things out of impoundment. If the person goes back on the property, he risks being arrested and put in jail. He can have nothing now to do with the property. The bank is now in possession of the property.

The reason I have gone through this step by step, is to show the gruesome side of the process. I want to find these properties long before they get to the sale. I have stood on the sidewalk watching a young family with their three children lose their house. They thought they could save the house. They could not. They just kept ignoring the announcements and then, there they were, standing on the sidewalk in tears, the little kids were allowed to keep their bigwheels because the Sheriff's deputies were nice. I stood there on the sidewalk and cried with this family. It was really sad. I realized then that if I could be more persuasive in talking to people, I could get them to understand that I was willing to give them a little bit of money, at least enough to get them set up in another place, and save their credit rating.

Now, on the time line, where do you fit in? If you could find out about this property before the announcements are sent out–in the beginning when the people are just starting to get the late payment notices, and if they realized they could not make up the back payments, they might be willing to sell it to you, rather than lose the house. If they knew that they were not going to be able to cure it, then this is one point where you could come into the picture.

Another entry point would be after the house is already in some state of foreclosure, but before the cure date. The only way to do it then is to deal with the attorney or the representative of the bank who is handling the sale. You may come into the time line after the cure date only by attending the auction.

There are obviously better places than others to come into the picture. In the later chapters, we will see how to get there first and how to process things before they ever get to the state of being auctioned off.

Publisher's Note

Available now is the complete *Pre-Foreclosure System* on four hours of cassette tapes. It also contains all the forms, documents and explanations that will help you establish your own step-by-step system of getting foreclosure properties before the auction. This is the most definitive foreclosure system available today. You can order this system by calling:

Wade Cook Seminars, Inc.
14675 Interurban Avenue South
Seattle, Washington 98168
206-901-3000

Ask for the *Pre-Foreclosures System* cassette tape set. Mastercard, Visa, and American Express card holders may call 1-800-872-7411 and ask for the *Pre-Foreclosures System* cassette tape set.

Excerpt from "How To Pick Up Foreclosures"

THE ACTUAL TIME LINE

AUCTION — cure date

calm before the storm

legal notices start

letters form attorney

letters from bank

PROBLEM STARTS

Months	1	2	3	4	5	6	7	8	9
Monthly Payment	$700	$700	$700	$700	$700	$700	$700	$700	NO
Late Payment	30	30	30	30	30	30	30	30	NO
Foreclosure Costs			50	25	100	100	50	50	NO
Total to Cure	$730	$1,460	$2,240	$2,995	$3,825	$4,655	$5,425	$6,215	$6,215

This example depicts the urgency of stopping the foreclosure proceedings in its early stages. The earlier stopped, the better the leverage.

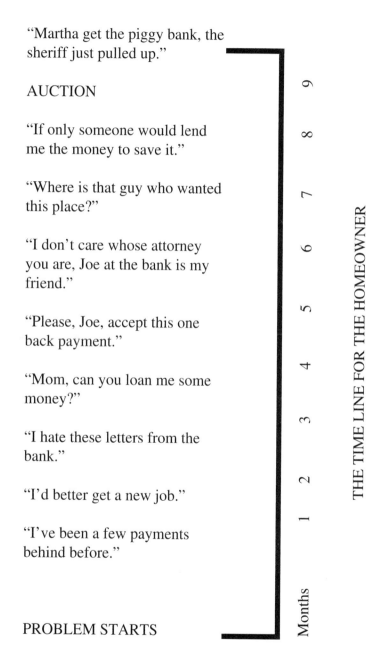

"Martha get the piggy bank, the sheriff just pulled up."

AUCTION

"If only someone would lend me the money to save it."

"Where is that guy who wanted this place?"

"I don't care whose attorney you are, Joe at the bank is my friend."

"Please, Joe, accept this one back payment."

"Mom, can you loan me some money?"

"I hate these letters from the bank."

"I'd better get a new job."

"I've been a few payments behind before."

PROBLEM STARTS

THE TIME LINE FOR THE HOMEOWNER

9 8 7 6 5 4 3 2 1

Months

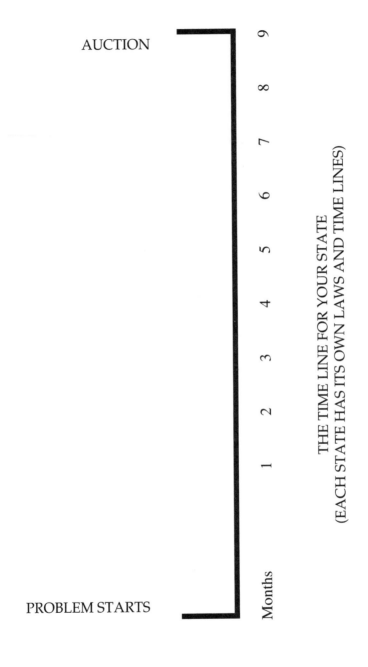

Contents from "How To Pick Up Foreclosures"

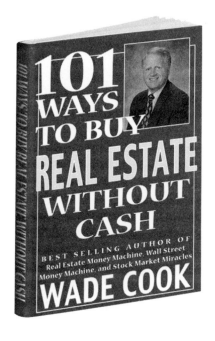

Section 2

Seller Accepts Low Or No Money Down Deals

When you plan to make an offer on a property, you naturally want to get the best deal for your money, but so does the seller. In this section, you will learn some secrets of negotiation so you will be ahead in the long run and have a satisfied seller. Your seller may have different plans than you do, but as you negotiate and show that it's in his best interest to accept a "no" or "low-money" down deal, he will wrap his mind around your offer as he understands the benefits of doing so. Put the seller in the driver's seat and let them make their own decisions.

Who do you think is the best person to make decisions for you when you're getting ready to buy a house? You are! And who do you think has a lot of great ideas about the price, terms and curb appeal of a house? You do! So, who do you want to have making the choices and decisions about the purchase of a house? Well, naturally, you do. And so does the seller. Keep this in mind as you prepare your offer; don't give them just one offer—give them three! They like to be in control of the sale just as much as you do, so prepare your three best offers, giving and taking, and negotiate from there. This section will give you several scenarios of how I did just that.

Total Owner Carryback

1

Suppose you find a property you would like to acquire with a fair market value (FMV) of $50,000. It has an existing assumable mortgage of $30,000 at 8% interest per year, with payments of $245 per month. The seller's equity in the house is $20,000.

You offer the seller the basic no money down deal. You tell him, "I like your house very much and I really want to buy it. It's worth $50,000, and I'm willing to give you that much for it. But I can't give you that much all at once. I can do this, though. I can go ahead and assume your mortgage for $30,000 with the bank. I'll start making these payments to the bank immediately. I know that you have $20,000 worth of equity in the house over and above your mortgage. I can pay you this $20,000 for your equity and buy your house if you will let me pay it off in monthly payments. I'll give you a $20,000 second mortgage on the house at 11% interest per year. I will be making monthly payments of $200 to you."

At first, the seller is shocked by your offer. He says, "I want my $20,000 now! I can't afford to wait around and let that $20,000 dribble in at a rate of $200 a month!"

You reply, "There are three reasons why you might rather have this paid off in monthly payments as opposed to getting the $20,000 all at once. The first reason is that you could save yourself a lot of money on taxes."

His eyes light up with real interest at the mention of the word taxes. "How would it save me money on taxes?"

You explain, "If I pay you $20,000 cash right now, you have to declare the whole thing on your income taxes for this year. Do you know how much tax you would have to pay on that? It would probably jump you into a higher tax bracket, too, so you would be paying a higher percentage on your regular income for the year, as well as the $20,000 extra for the sale of your house."

"You're right," he says. "There really would be a big advantage as far as taxes are concerned. What are the other two reasons you mentioned?"

You continue, "This will give you a regular steady monthly income.

You can use this steady monthly income to help you with your retirement, or use it to buy something you want—a car, or furniture, or anything else you would like. You could use these monthly payments to make monthly payments on something else you would like to buy."

"That's true," he admits. "It would be nice to have a steady monthly income."

"And the third reason is this: this money will not pay off quickly. At $200 per month, I will be making these payments to you for twenty years or more. You will end up with far more money in the long run than if I gave you $20,000 cash right now. You will end up with something more like $60,000 than $20,000."

He makes his decision. "All right, you've got yourself a deal."

Congratulations! You've just bought a house with no money down!

This is really the ultimate in no down payment financing. It is called the "paper-out." The name comes from the simple reason that the seller wants to "get out" of his property so desperately that he is willing to take a note, or "paper" from you, with no down payment in the form of cash.

Why would any seller do this? You can rest assured that he has a very pressing reason for selling the property. He is called a "Don't-Wanter." This is the term used to describe a highly motivated seller. He has some kind of ownership problem. When you come to him with your offer, you will replace his ownership problem with a steady positive cash flow from your paper.

You can sometimes even do better than this, and set up the deal so that you will not be making any monthly payments at all for awhile. The secret is all in negotiation.

The Wraparound Mortgage

2

You answer an ad in the newspaper and find a single family dwelling for sale by owner. It has a fair market value of $60,000 with an existing assumable first mortgage of $30,000 at 8% interest, with payments of

Excerpt from "101 Ways To Buy Real Estate Without Cash"

$245 per month. The seller's equity is $20,000.

You meet with the owner and present your program. You offer to pay the full $50,000. You agree to assume the first mortgage and begin making payments right away. Then you offer a second mortgage to the seller for the $20,000 equity in the house, and offer to pay $200 a month at 10% interest.

This would give you total monthly payments of $445: the $200 per month to the seller and $245 per month to the bank on the first mortgage.

At this point, the seller might be a bit dubious, and say, "What if something happens and you start missing payments on the first mortgage to the bank? Then the bank might foreclose and I would lose my house."

You make him another offer. "As long as you are still making payments in your first mortgage with the bank, you feel secure, right? You know the bank is not going to foreclose on you."

The seller nods. "As long as I'm the one who is making the payments, I know the payments are always going to be made and I know I'm not going to lose the house to the bank."

"Then let's do this," you say. "You continue to make your regular payments to the bank on the first mortgage, and I will make all my monthly payments directly to you. I'll give you what they call a wraparound mortgage."

"A wraparound mortgage? What is that?"

"It works like this," you say. "I'm buying your house at a price of $50,000. I'll give you a mortgage on the whole $50,000, and make you payments of $445 per month, at a 10% rate of interest. This way, I will be paying the same amount of money that I would have paid to you and to the bank together, only this way, I will pay the whole $445 to you. Then you can take $245 out of that every month and pay the bank your own monthly payments on your first mortgage. As long as you are making your payments to the bank, you'll never have to worry about the bank foreclosing on you."

The seller understands what you're talking about now. To him, that sounds like a much better arrangement. You tell the seller, "On the surface, you appear to be getting the same deal as far as the money is concerned. But in reality you are getting a much better deal than that."

"Really?" asks the seller, "How much better?"

You sit down at the table with him and start putting figures down on a piece of paper. "Let's look at the actual affect here. I'm paying you $5,000 per year in interest. That is 10% of $50,000 per year. You are netting the difference of $2,600 per year. Your equity is $20,000, so you are actually netting 13% per year on this transaction. $2,600 is 13% of $20,000, and that is the equity you are receiving the interest on."

He studies the figures on the paper. "That's right," he says, "and that's a higher interest rate than 10%. What's happening here?"

"Just this. I'm paying you 10% interest per year on the entire $50,000 value of your house. But you don't actually own $50,000 worth of this house! You actually own only $20,000 worth of equity in this house. The bank owns the other $30,000. That means I am paying you 10% interest on the $30,000 worth of your house still owned by the bank."

You go on. "You are paying off your first mortgage with the bank at a much faster rate than my wraparound mortgage of $50,000 to you. This means that your equity, which is starting out at $20,000 right now, is actually going to be growing in value each year. When your first mortgage is paid off in 15 years or so, my wraparound mortgage to you will still have an unpaid balance of about $35,000!"

The seller studies the figures on the paper in front of him. He finally says, "This isn't a good deal. This is a great deal!"

This is really a win/win transaction for you *and* the seller.

The Fixer-Upper: A Great Nothing Down Deal   3

The very fact that a house is a fixer-upper means it is a natural to become a nothing down deal. The owner really knows what condition the house is in, and he wants to sell it "as is." He knows someone is going to have to spend the money required for repairs. He also knows that he does not want to have to be the one spending that money. Or maybe he doesn't have the money to make the necessary repairs.

So you come along and present your offer. "Mr. Jones, I know that you want $2,000 down for your property, but your home really does

Excerpt from "101 Ways To Buy Real Estate Without Cash"

need some fixing up, and I just don't have enough money to make the down payment and still fix the house up the way it should be. I'll need to keep all the money I have in order to fix up the house after I buy it."

"If you let me use my $2,000 to fix this place up instead of on a down payment, it's going to be worth a lot more than it is right now. This will raise the actual value of the property, and there will be more equity in it above the mortgage you have on it right now."

You continue, "This will make your position much more secure. After I spend my money to fix the place up and the equity is increased, I will own that extra equity. This means that if I ever stop making payments to you, you can go ahead and foreclose on the house, and I will lose all my equity as well as the house. I would have more to lose if I lost the house, and you would have more to gain if you got the house back."

Think about this. Would you rather spend your money on someone else's equity, or fix up the property and gain equity of your own? When you use your money to fix up that property, you are gaining equity; usually more equity, dollar for dollar, than the money you are actually spending on it.

I do not like spending my cash for someone else's equity. I will trade in my cash to buy potential, but not the other person's equity. When someone says he has equity in his property, that is his problem. I'm not going to give him cash for his equity. I would rather keep my cash and go out and buy something I really want, like a TV, car or computer.

Cash for equity is not a fair trade. You trade something that is very liquid for something that is not. If you put cash into a property, you had better be figuring out a way to get that cash back when you want it.

Never put yourself in a position where you are short of cash.

Contents

from "101 Ways To Buy Real Estate Without Cash"

what was already available to any college student, the young man decided to write a book about his Money Machine concept, and start teaching people how to retire using the Real Estate Money Machine...

As he wrote and taught, our young man saw many, many people take his Money Machine concept and become wealthy. They achieved their dreams—some retired, some put their children through college without hardship, some became active in their communities with the extra time their money could buy them. He was very happy to share his formula and see his students succeed.

But he also found that some people came to his seminars and did not succeed. He wondered what was missing; what was the difference between those who learned and applied their new knowledge and those who learned and simply sat on their learning? He began to think that perhaps there was a design to success, a set of blueprints that anyone could follow to build a successful life. He pulled together some of the students who had succeeded tremendously with his principles and asked them to write about what they knew and had learned about success...

(Continued on page 105)

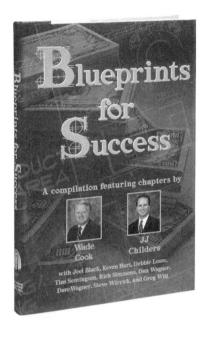

A Strategy For Success

Steve Wirrick

 ome of the questions I love to ask people at our seminars are: "What are you looking for when you invest? You have taken time out of your day to come and spend it with us. Why? What are you wanting out of this information?" What has been interesting to me is that overwhelmingly, the same three basic answers keep coming back.

So to get started, I'd love to share those with you because it will lay the foundation for everything we'll discuss in these special reports.

The number one reason why people invest, and I don't care whether it's in the stock market, real estate, a business, or a franchise, is for the CASH FLOW. Obviously, that comes as no surprise. People want more money. In fact, how

> **The darkest hour of any man's life is when he sits down to plan how to get money without earning it.**
>
> *Horace Greeley*

many of you find that you always have way more month than you do money?

The second reason why people invest is for tax write offs. They are sick and tired of working four months out of the year for Uncle Sam before they see a dime. They want to keep more of their money right in their own home, businesses, communities and churches.

> It is not the return on my investment that I am concerned about; it is the return *of* my investment.
>
> *Will Rogers*

The final reason why people invest is for GROWTH—the appreciation of the asset, so they and their families can have something to retire on. They want to stop trading time for money.

Furthermore, people want all three of those things at the same time, and they also want to get started with very little money.

What I find interesting is that real estate is one of only two investments that I know of where you can do just that. Where you can get cash flow, tax write-offs and growth, get them all at the same time and get started with very little money. In fact, with real estate you can still get started with no money.

Well, that begs the question, besides real estate, what's the other investment? Do you have any guesses? Stocks? Bonds? Options? REITs?

Let's put the stock market to the test, because here we are talking about the stock market—it has to fit our formula, right? Well, let's put it to the test and see what happens.

Cash Flow

When we invest in the stock market, are we always generating cash flow? No we don't. Uh-oh, we already have a problem. Now, if you buy-sell, buy-sell, hopefully you are, but let me ask you a question. Do you own stocks? Do you receive dividends on a quarterly, semi-annually, or annualized basis? If you know, what is the yield of those dividends? Pretty low, isn't it?! The average yield of all publicly traded companies is about 3 to 5%. The yield on the Standard and Poor's 500 is at a historic low right now—1.7%. Now if you're looking to get rich at 1.7% a year, is it going to happen? It's like we're on a slow boat going nowhere. In fact, if I mix in a little inflation of about 3% per year, are we going forwards or backwards? We actually may be losing ground!

Tax Write offs

If you have tax write offs in the stock market, what's that saying? Ugh, we're losing money. Ouch! Do you hate losing money? We all do. You can make $8,000 in a week, lose $600 on another play and it ruins the whole week. Did we make money? Sure we did, but you don't like losing money. I don't like losing money. So, how about latching ourselves onto strategies, a plan, a system, a way that will prevent us and keep us from losing money? It is definitely easier said than done. In fact, my special reports deal with just that.

> If you are truly serious about preparing your child for the future, don't teach him to subtract–teach him to deduct.
>
> *Fran Lebowitz*

Growth

Do stocks always go up? No they don't. They have a tendency to go down.

As you can see, the stock market has a hard time delivering on any one of these items, let alone all three at the same time. So what does?

Well, here's my curve ball for you. The only other investment I know of besides real estate that gives us CASH FLOW, TAX WRITE OFFS AND GROWTH, gives it to us all at the same time, and where we can still get started with very little money, is simply by running and operating your own small business. My own small business? Yes, your own small business. Now, stick with me here because it's critical to your trading style and lays the foundation upon which it is based.

Cash Flow

I would say the number one reason why people go into business for themselves is because they want more cash flow. They are sick and tired of working for somebody else. They hate having a boss breathing down their necks. They want to get paid what they are really worth. They want to call the shots. Having your own business provides such an opportunity.

Tax Write offs

If you had your own small business, you get more tax deductions than an individual. In fact, has Congress done a pretty good job of wiping out deductions for investment purposes? Yes, they have. But, if we do something for business purposes, can we still write that off? Yes! Are there things right now that we spend money on as individuals that we can't write off; but that if your business would buy it, we could write it off? You bet! What are some of those things? Car, gas, insurance, and computers to name a few. In fact, that's why I love the seminar business, because instead of taking vacations, we're going to start taking what kind of trips? Business trips! Man, I love it. Now if you run into the beach, pool, or Mickey Mouse on your way to the business seminar, can you write it off? Talk to your accountant and they can bring you up to speed on how to set that up properly. The point is: do more in the name of business. Many of us overpay, that's right, overpay our taxes because we don't take advantage of all the deductions available to us. We can't get to where we want to be—financially independent if we keep sharing 40% of what we make with someone else.

> Collecting more taxes than is absolutely necessary is legalized robbery.
>
> *Calvin Coolidge*

Growth

Hopefully you're building a business for the future. So what's my point? My point is this:

If we are looking for cash flow, tax write offs and growth in our investments, and we are getting the same cash flow, tax write offs and growth by running and operating our own small businesses, why don't we marry those two things together. We need to start treating our investments like a business! I don't want that to slip by you as just another cute statement. It is powerful! It is key to your success. Start treating your investments like a business and watch your cash flow sky-rocket. Why? Because right now we have a tendency to do the exact opposite. We don't treat our investments like a business.

Let's take a look at a typical retail business so I can show you what I mean. A business makes money by buying wholesale and selling retail. They buy in order to sell. But what have we been taught to do in the stock market? We buy and hold. Now, don't get me wrong. I'm not saying that you should sell all of your investments. I'm not saying you can't build up a nice portfolio. But think in terms of running your business like that. Someone walks into your store and wants to purchase something. You look them straight in the eye and say, "I can't sell you anything. We buy and hold in this store. We hold our inventory." I'm being facetious, but my point is a valid one. There's no money made until something is sold. Now, don't get me wrong. I love buying assets, but for many of us that's for the birds right now. Why? Because you are buying and holding instead of buying and selling! Can you be asset rich, yet cash poor? You better believe it! That's where a lot of us are in life. We have a bunch of stuff that looks good on paper, but we can't pay the bills. In fact, what buys the assets in the first place? If you bought a stock at $10 and it's trading at $100 today, have you made any money? No. Now, don't get me wrong, it looks great on paper but the last time I checked you couldn't buy groceries on margin. You can't put stock certificates in the gas tank. Can you quit your job? No. We're asset rich and cash poor. It's the cash flow that enables you to quit your job. It's the cash flow that enables you to take a vacation. It's the cash flow that pays for the kid's piano lessons, not the assets.

Let's go one step further. How many of you work for someone else? How long would it be before your income stops if you don't go to work? Perhaps you have your own business? How long before your business goes out of business if you don't go in to your place of business, your shop, your warehouse?

What I'm alluding to is an income producing asset. For many of us, we are it. If our asset doesn't go to work, when does our income stop? Immediately.

> **Business is like riding a bicycle. Either you keep moving or you fall down.**
>
> *American business saying*

99

Excerpt from "Blueprints for Success"

I have a proposition for you. How about making it our goal to replace ourselves as the income producing asset, so the income keeps coming in whether we go to work or not. You could be at the beach, by the pool, or fast asleep in bed, and the money doesn't stop. Interested?

That's our goal. The American Dream. Financial Independence. Doing what you want, when you want to do it. What does that mean to you? Time with the kids, no debt, taking a trip around the world, or fixing up the car? Whatever it means to you, that is your goal!

In order to get you there, I need you to change your mindset just a little bit. By doing so, you'll open the window to so many possibilities financially. It'll blow your mind!

I need you to scrape together whatever cash you can. I need you to dump it into an asset. But instead of stopping there, and holding onto it like we are used to doing, I need you to get back to CASH! As quickly as possible. And that is our mantra: CASH - ASSET - CASH—the quicker the better. If you can do it in three weeks, great! In one day, fantastic! Better yet, how about within the hour? What it comes down to is treating your investments like a business. We buy in order to sell. The quicker the better!

> Do you know the only thing that gives me pleasure? It's to see my dividends coming in.
>
> *John D. Rockefeller*

When you start thinking like that, you will be able to make unbelievable amounts of cash. How about turning $300 into $1,200? Or, making an extra $1,200 to $2,500 a month? How about earning $40,000 a month or more! It's all possible if you take the time to learn how to do it. It's that simple!

When you consider the unbelievable amounts of money you can make and how quickly you can make it trading options, you may ask yourself, "Why aren't more people doing this? If this is so great, wonderful and true, why haven't my brokers told me about it?"

Those are great questions, but too easy for me to answer, so, let me throw it back at you. If this is so great, wonderful and true, why aren't more people doing it?

I get varied responses, but ultimately they revolve around three areas, or "walls" as I like to call them. I call them walls because there are barriers in our lives that prevent us from getting what we want. If you could identify what the wall or walls are that are holding you back, would that have value? Yes! See, when we know what the walls are that are holding us back, we can then destroy them. What are those walls?

The biggest wall for most people is a lack of knowledge. "If I knew more about options, I could make money with them." Most people have never been taught anything regarding options. How can I expect it of you, or you expect it of yourself, to do something that you didn't know existed? Can you gain knowledge quickly? Yes, you can. And I don't mean just any kind of knowledge, I mean specialized knowledge. If you dig for oil where there's oil, what will you find? Oil! So, if you specialize in knowledge that makes money, what will you make? Money!

> If money is your hope for independence, you will never have it. The only real security that a man can have in this world is a reserve of knowledge, experience, and ability.
>
> *Henry Ford*

You can have a lot of knowledge about something, but what else holds us back? Fear or what I will call a lack of confidence. A lack of confidence is another wall for many people.

What do you think the scariest trade of all will be? That's right! Your first one. It was the same for everyone who has ever traded. Just like the first date, first day on the job, or the first time riding a bike. How did we conquer the fear? By doing it! What makes it a lot easier is knowing what to do, when to do it, and what to say. That increases your confidence. These reports will take you by the hand and lead you around the mines found in the minefield of options trading. Do you want to go it alone or with someone who has been across many a time?

You can have a lot of knowledge about something, and you can be full of confidence, but what else do we need to get started? Money! It is the lack of money that acts as the third wall for many people.

At our seminars across the country, people tell me all the time that they love what they learned, but they don't have any money to get started. My response is, "If you don't get some money together, will you be able to do what I'm showing you?" No. And if you continue to do what you have always done, what will you continue to get?

Excerpt from "Blueprints for Success"

Nothing.

The definition of crazy that I really love is: if you continue to do what you've always done but expect different results. Now, that's crazy!!

So, the question really becomes, not whether or not you have the money, but where are you going to get it? Because, if you don't get it, you can't get started. And if you can't get started, you are left with what you have. And that's what we're trying to change! We want more out of life: more money! More time with our kids!

Let me share with you a little secret: if you take time to learn how money is made, what will you start doing? Making money! If you don't take time to learn how money is made, what will be the result? Nothing. Are you telling me that knowledge is the answer?! It sure is! It's knowledge that makes you money. It's knowledge that gives us confidence by knowing what to do, and when to do it. Knowledge is key!

The American Dream is alive and well if you but take the time to learn how to get it.

The American Dream is alive and well if you but take the time to learn how to get it.

Congratulations on taking the first step!!

● ● ●

Learn from Steve Wirrick how you can succeed just as he has! Call **1-800-872-7411** and ask for *The HIT Pack*, Steve's audio home study course.

102

Contents
from "Blueprints for Success"

From these people and from his personal upbringing and study, the man started to sort out his own principles of success. He looked at the ideas contained in the many, many books available about goal setting, time management, self improvement and affirmations, and contrasted them with the actions and thinking that had led to his own phenomenal success. He began to see where our energy goes to sap our success instead of feeding it.

The man continued to be successful in real estate and as a seminar speaker teaching people how to make money as he did. He knew he did not want to put his excess money from all this success into savings accounts—he wanted a much higher rate of return. Instead, he began to invest in second mortgages, stocks and mutual funds.

The second mortgages did well, since real estate was a field he knew. The stocks and mutual funds, on the other hand, were a new arena for him. He read and studied and learned what he could about the stock market, and it seemed everything centered around a single strategy—buy stock and wait for it to appreciate. The problem was, the stocks and funds he bought seemed to DE-preciate before they A-ppreciated. He

(Continued on page 111)

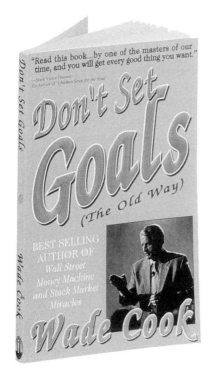

4:
Direction

"In my company I'll give my back forty acres for a loyal, enthusiastic person."

—Wade Cook

I have a good friend named Nick. He flies for a major airline and also has a tropical flower farm in Hawaii. He is very astute and not only a thinker, but a doer, a rare mixture of qualities.

We met at one of my seminars, and though I don't become close friends with many of my attendees, I, actually we, as my wife joined in, have become friends with Nick and his wife, Judi.

I invited Nick to be on the Board of Directors of our parent company, which is publicly traded. He has served with dedication and exuberance. I have enjoyed his ideas, his feedback, his caring, and concern.

We have many discussions, usually about the Bible, but often on business. I mentioned in one of my seminars that direction was more important than speed, because Nick loves to fly and it shows.

I asked him about getting off course and the corrections necessary to correct problems. The scenario was a flight from Los Angeles to

New York. A small error, left uncorrected, a wind change or other traffic could put the plane off course. If uncorrected for a long period of time the results would be dramatic.

Even a very small degree change, if prolonged, would leave the plane way off course. I know this would never happen, but imagine the New York bound plane ending up in Washington D.C. or Boston. They are hundreds of miles from New York. But from Los Angeles, a slight shift would take you over Riverside instead of San Bernardino.

The angle is the key. A large degree variance has an exponential effect later. I mean, the plane could end up in Miami. On the other hand, the problem at the beginning is simple to correct, with the right instruments and right people.

Think of the cost of correcting a major mistake. The fuel from Washington, D.C. back to New York is costly. Think of the angry passengers. Now, I know this won't happen, but the point, I hope, is made.

In life, as in business, we need to constantly make corrections. If the direction is good in the first place, if we still want the intended results, then all sorts of things will arise to help and hinder the process.

But give me a man or woman with a mission, and it's as if the very forces of nature will lie down to allow the accomplishment of the task.

A person with a mission, a passion and enthusiasm, is a sight to behold. In my company I'll give my back forty acres for a loyal, enthusiastic person. You can measure the success of the direction you're going by how well your passion is sustained. If it wanes, then check your integrity level. Is what you say, do, and think, all the same? Keep this in alignment.

By saying direction is more important than speed, I do not mean to imply that speed is not important. One maxim I've used at my seminars and in other books is this,

"If you'll do for two years what most people <u>won't</u> do, you'll be able to do for the rest of your life what most people <u>can't</u> do."

In our fast paced society, our attention span has decreased. If you read my financial books you'll hear me talk about "two years" quite often. For example, I have a web site where I list almost all of my trades, plus our instructors trades and dozens of other information tips. Through our website, people can subscribe to **WIN** (Wealth Information Network) for this information. We sell the package by the year. Many of our students subscribe to WIN so they can look over the shoulder of a millionaire and his staff. It's a very popular service, but I tell them, "Okay, buy one year, maybe two, but if you haven't gotten rich in that time using my formulas, you'll probably never make it. Go do something else."

If you go about a task and you don't see results right away, you'll probably get discouraged and quit. That's why speed and results are important.

My daughter gets a lot of feedback, results, and ribbons on her way to Youth Nationals. I don't know how she or anyone can achieve great things without feeling a sense of accomplishment.

I'm reminded of a story learned long ago about the woman trying to swim the English Channel. The day she set out was very foggy. After a few miles she tired and quit. On a clear day, when she could see way out, she made it.

Goals, tasks, or targets have to be definable, achievable and then done with adequate speed in the proper direction.

"Get" to the financial goals you've already "set!"
Choose your FREE cassette and send in the postcard on
the back flap or call **1-800-872-7411** and ask about our
FREE seminar on tape to get you started!

Contents

from "Don't Set Goals"

began to feel frustrated and impatient with this same old conventional wisdom. It was at about this time his stock broker friend gave him the suggestion, and he applied the real estate principals to the stock market.

The stock market courses continued to grow, as did the man's wealth and his company. But there were still people who avoided him, avoided his books and seminars, and even avoided hearing anything that could help them create the lives they dreamed of. He wondered again why some people seem to resist success, to disbelieve that they too are capable of reaching their goals.

Again he studied, asked questions, and inquired into what he had learned that maybe these others had not been taught. He began to see that some people think wealth and prosperity are not spiritual; that good people are usually poor people. He decided to do his own research and wrote a new book on what the Bible really says about prosperity. He called it *Business Buy The Bible...*

(Continued on page 127)

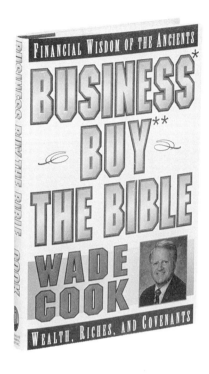

*Fear not, little flock;
for it is your Father's good plea-
sure to give you the kingdom.*
Luke 12:32

Back To
The Ancients

It started with Adam. He had all he needed. In fact, he lived a life of abundance. Nothing was lacking. So, we can literally say that God has provided financial prosperity for those who are obedient to Him from the beginning of time. Adam chose to sin and the results, along with being deprived of spiritual things, produced a loss of abundance. Poverty entered the picture.

This setting is our basis. As we move on to Abraham, we will find many useful statements, lessons, and ideas to help solidify in our hearts and minds God's will towards us. Let's use James as our theme:

17   **Every good gift and every perfect gift is from above, and cometh down from the Father of Lights, with whom is no variableness, neither shadow of turning.**

                                            James 1:17

The Lord appeared to Abram when he was quite old. We'll list the encounter here:

1   And when Abram was ninety years old and nine, the Lord appeared to Abram, and said unto him, I am the Almighty God; walk before me, and be thou perfect.

2   And I will make my covenant between me and thee, and will multiply thee exceedingly.

3   And Abram fell on his face: and God talked with him, saying,

4   As for me, behold, my covenant is with thee, and thou shalt be a father of many nations.

5   Neither shall thy name any more be called Abram, but thy name shall be Abraham; for a father of many nations I have made thee.

6   And I will make thee exceedingly fruitful, and I will make nations of thee, and kings shall come out of thee.

7   And I will establish my covenant between me and thee and thy seed after thee in their generations for an everlasting covenant, to be a God unto thee and to thy seed after thee.

8   And I will give unto thee, and to thy seed after thee, the land wherein thou art a stranger, all the land of Canaan, for an everlasting possession; and I will be their God.

9   And God said unto Abraham, Thou shalt keep my covenant therefore, thou, and thy seed after thee in their generations.

Genesis 17:1-9

There is one little word in verses seven and eight that is of particular interest to me. It is the word "and." Look at the use of it the third and fourth time it is used and the second and third time in verse eight and the second time it is used in verse nine. In fact, the Lord uses this word "and" quite frequently in his dealings with Abraham. It is used to include "his seed," or his posterity. His seed is to be included in this awesome covenant and promise.

We can read about this great covenant and see how it applies to Abram, now called Abraham, but is that it? And for how many more generations does the covenant apply to his seed? And even if it extends down through many generations, what does it mean for you and me?

Verses seven and nine say it applies "in their generations." The word is plural. Okay, but are we a part of his seed? Do we qualify if we fulfill our part of this covenant ("walk before me, and be thou perfect" [verse 1], "keep my covenant" [verse 9])?

We need to explore this covenant and in particular, certain aspects of it which deal with prosperity, but let's continue in this qualifying vein to see how we are a part. Why be concerned about its true meaning to us unless we are one of the generations which can be a part of the covenant blessing?

Internal to the covenant of Abraham are all of the blessings (if obedient) and the curses (if disobedient). God gave it His all. It was complete. He was even willing to give His Son: "He that spared not his own Son, but delivered him up for us all, how shall he not with him also freely give us all things?" (Roman 8:32) The covenant contained all, including Jesus. Jesus could not only fulfill the law, he could make it better. He can make the promises, the greatest which is God being our God, extend beyond this earth. Hebrews 8:6 says: "But now hath he obtained a more excellent ministry, by how much also he is the mediator of a better covenant, which was established upon better promises." This better covenant was brought about "in the blood" of Jesus. Look again at a part, albeit an extensive part, of the covenant as explained in Hebrews:

13   **For when God made promise to Abraham, because
      He could swear by no greater, He sware by Himself,**

14 Saying, Surely blessing I will bless thee, and
multiplying I will multiply thee.

Hebrews 6:13-14

(Note that God could not swear by anyone greater than Himself,
because He is the greatest. "He sware by Himself.")

32 **And we declare unto you glad tidings, how that
the promise which was made unto the fathers,**
33 **God hath fulfilled the same unto us their children,
in that he hath raised up Jesus again; as it is
also written in the second Psalm, Thou art my
Son, this day have I begotten thee.**

Acts 13:32-33

God is sure. He fulfilled his promises. Throughout the generations
(if the people are obedient and true to His word) His covenant is
established.

The last time I asked you to look at verse seven in the seventeenth
chapter of Genesis, it was to point out the "ands." It was to show how
future generations could participate in this Abrahamic covenant.
Now, let's use that same verse to go back to ancient times once again.

"I will establish," are God's words. He did not want someone else
to do it. This was a special arrangement: a promise with exceedingly
great ramifications.

God seems to deal with his people through covenants: two-way
promises. There is something in a covenant for both parties. Here He
says, "I will establish," or make sure, make steadfast, put on a firm
basis. In the next verse He ends with, "and I will be their God."

Between these two statements, He gives them land. That means a
lot. With land they can prosper with flocks, and plants, and also have
the security land brings. Even to this day, the people who trace their

lineage to Abraham are still fighting over that land. And what happened? Abraham became great, meaning an abundance of riches:

35   **And the Lord hath blessed my master greatly, and
        he is become great: and he hath given him flocks,
        and herds, and silver, and gold, and menservants,
        and maidservants, and camels, and asses.**

                                        Genesis 24:35

This was spoken by a servant of Abraham. Later in that same chapter, this servant was sent on a mission and before he left, he questioned: "And I said unto my master, Peradventure the woman will not follow me? (What if she will not follow me?)" He was told to say: "The Lord, before whom I walk, will send his angel with thee, and prosper thy way; and thou shalt take a wife for my son of my kindred, and of my father's house." (Genesis 24:39-40)

In his early days, before the covenant was established, Abraham was blessed. He was following the commandments of the Lord: "And Abram was very rich in cattle, in silver, and in gold." (Genesis 13:2)

Now, let's take a brief look at the covenant working in future generations:

5   **And Abraham gave all that he had unto Isaac.**

                                        Genesis 25:5

(Quick political note: Will all those who tax read this passage? Isaac didn't have to pay an estate or inheritance tax on what his father passed on to him. Please take note and eliminate these taxes.)

11   **And it came to pass after the death of Abraham,
        that God blessed his son Isaac; and Isaac dwelt by
        the well Lahai-roi.**

                                        Genesis 25:11

Excerpt from "Business Buy The Bible"

God had said he would continue his covenant with all the seed of Abraham. Let's look at His appearance to Isaac:

24 And the Lord appeared unto him the same night, and said, I am the God of Abraham thy father: fear not, for I am with thee, and will bless thee, and multiply thy seed for my servant Abraham's sake.

Genesis 26:24

Wow! Here are the blessings coming to life again. Look at a few scriptures that we'll list here and explain in other parts of this book:

12 Then Isaac sowed in that land, and received in the same year an hundredfold: and the Lord blessed him.
13 And the man waxed great, and went forward, and grew until he became very great: [*Note: The word "great" here probably could be replaced with rich. When the word "great" is used, it is usually followed by a listing of assets.*]
14 For he had possession of flocks, and posses-sion of herds, and great store of servants: and the Philistines envied him.

Genesis 26:12-14

Scriptural evidence shows we are meant to prosper. All it takes is living in accord with spiritual principles. Call for the *SAIL* package–*Scriptural Applications In Life*–and start achieving the wealth you were meant to have.
1-800-872-7411

Contents

from "Business Buy The Bible"

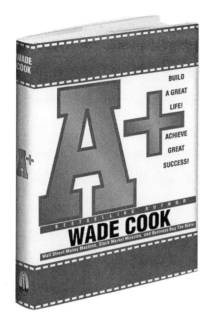

3

The highest earthly enjoyments are but a shadow of the joy I find in reading God's word.

—Lady Jane Grey

Enthusiasm

When a new business or investment book hits the market, I buy it. I have quite a collection. I constantly look for new ideas, new methods, or little how to's which can make big differences. There are, and will continue to be thousands of management books in the bookstores at any given time. I buy many of them. If I want ideas on agenda planning or meeting structures, or if I want budgeting and cash flow management techniques, I can quickly lay my hands on dozens, if not hundreds, of ideas.

However, in my daily watching and running of my own business (which I feel is superbly successful), or watching other successful businesses, I find something lacking in virtually all of these books. This something—the key to success—is overlooked by authors. This is strange. Most of these authors are successful business *consultants*, and they have missed what made their own business a success. I know because I have talked to them. They are successful because they have enthusiasm, not because of their product or service.

Contents from "A+"

These people come to my seminars. They learn so much in our *Wall Street Workshop* that they themselves are astonished. Many make $20,000 to $30,000 within a month, and then even share my techniques with their clients. Their clients soon come to one of my workshops.

When I find out about their businesses I see several things. One, their businesses are expanding, and they are usually trying to level out the peaks and valleys with steadier cash flow. Two, they have a specialty or a favorite method for helping other businesses. With this method, they are passionate. They have zeal unbounded. They are enthusiastic.

I keep talking to them about how they work with clients. They normally miss the point of what their client truly needs. This key has made them successful but they can't see the trees for the forest. Yes, maybe their new accounting system will help. Yes, getting control of receivables is important. Yes, a better use of floor space will delay the move to a more expensive building. The consultant has done his job by helping cut costs.

Yet, soon other problems arise and the consultant is summoned again. It's a weird cycle and it goes on everywhere. If the owner or general manager doesn't use an outside consultant, he is left to his own devices. The latest trick from a seminar or a cutting-edge management book technique is explored, partially used, and abandoned. But the fix that solves all problems—the cure to the big problem from which all others spring—isn't found.

Band-aids and more band-aids. You've heard that of every 100 business startups, 80% fail within their first year. It's amazing to me that 20% of businesses make it. I am convinced very few people know how to start, run, and build a great business, a business that will support the owner and the owner's kids, not be supported by him or them.

Again, every big-time successful business and every really successful person has the key. Why, again, do so many people miss it?

Chapter 3 Enthusiasm

Maybe it's so simple that it's overlooked because of its simplicity. Enthusiasm is what drives a person to take an idea and make a company, and it's that same enthusiasm that makes the company succeed.

Enthusiasm, passion, a love of something, a dedicated drive—call it whatever—it is the single common thread that runs through all success. Enthusiasm is, in fact, sine-qua-non to success.

Nothing is so contagious as enthusiasm.
—Edward George Bulwer-Lytton

To see how needed enthusiasm is, how powerful it is, just look at a company or a person's career when they lose their enthusiasm. Look what happens when other things get in the way. Take money for example; is it the living force behind these businesses and people? I dare say, no. Money is nice, but it only drives the attitude a small way. Most gigantic successes love what they are doing.

As a long-time speaker, and as the CEO of a seminar company, I cannot name one other company, either in size or in effectiveness, that matches Wade Cook Seminars, Inc. I personally get hundreds and even thousands of thank you letters and testimonials from customers whose lives have been enhanced in every area because of what we teach.

Yet, if we are good, it is because we love so much what we are doing. My love for helping people and my passion for this business let me tolerate the small negatives. My employees are also passionate and dedicated; they carry the torch well. Our enthusiasm helps us develop innovative solutions to problems that would otherwise bog us down.

Do you think we could have built a half billion dollar company in less than five years (starting with $3,000 and some old office furniture) if we did not love this work?

Contents from "A+"

Look at this verse:

> [16] *So then because thou art lukewarm, and neither cold nor hot, I will spue thee out of my mouth.*
>
> *Revelation 3:16*

Can you imagine where we would be if we did not get up every morning excited to improve, to change, to grow, to serve better? We get paid well for our seminars, but the money is not the driving force. I know, at first, it is to some of my employees. But they too eventually come around and get bitten by our dedication to excellence, our passion for sharing and caring, our strong desire to build something that outlasts all of us.

It's catchy. Our customers feel it. Our sales representatives are wonderful. Many make more in the stock market every month than their commission checks. They walk the walk. Very few have quit—even when their income from investments far exceeds their needs and wants. If you ask them why, they usually say they stay because of the excitement. Being around enthusiastic people all day helps them stay enthused in their own lives. Enthusiasm is catchy, and enthusiastic people are exciting to be around.

A few have retired (sometimes they retire two or three times a year!). They keep coming back. I continue to ask why. It's because of the camaraderie and the excitement. The real question for anyone in business or starting a business is this: what can I do to create passion and excitement?

The Greeks put the words "en" (with) and "theos" (God) together to get entheos, and from that we get enthuse and enthusiasm. Yes, a person can be without God and get excited about a track meet, or new product, or a football game. It's usually fleeting though.

What I am talking about is real, lasting enthusiasm. This type best comes from a belief in God, a hope in something beyond this world.

Show me a quiet, peaceful enthusiasm, one based on strong values and well-founded beliefs, and I will show you a winner.

This is the type of person who excels every day—who lives his or her life in the second mile, always doing extra. This is the person whose actions continually seek to help and build other people. It is from this type of service that great things happen and wonderful, fulfilling lives are built.

Now, extend this personality to a small group, then to other groups or a larger group, and then to a whole company, and the dynamics of greatness are in place.

I can tell countless stories of companies with and without passion. Remember IBM a few years ago. The morale was low. Inroads by competitors were eating up market share. Sales were down. The stock lost nearly half its value. Some of the best employees were starting up competing companies or going elsewhere to work. It looked hopeless.

I am not privy to things at IBM; I do not know what it was that turned their attitude around. I can surmise. Maybe they had research (new products) too long in the development process. Maybe they needed to get rid of a few bad apples. Maybe they needed one star product or one star salesperson. Turn around they did. After a 2:1 stock split, the stock is four to five times higher. Sales are up. Ads are new and reflect a new attitude. Whatever they did, it instilled a new enthusiasm into the company and greatness (once again) followed. There are thousands of similar examples.

One requirement for an A+ life is to continually
study and learn new things. Call Wade Cook
Seminars, Inc. at **1-800-872-7411** and ask about our
wide range of education opportunities!

Contents from "A+"

SECTION 3

Managing the Dream

The man and many of his students were tremendously successful. They had more cash flow than they had ever dreamed possible, through learning predictable, repeatable strategies in real estate and the stock market. Financial freedom was within their reach.

The students now had cash-producing assets and higher incomes than ever before. This led to a whole new set of problems. They soon discovered that sometimes the hardest part of being wealthy isn't making money, but keeping it.

The successful students found their new income created a problem with higher income taxes. In addition, their high net worth caused them to be more liable to lawsuits. Lawyers will often counsel a client to pursue a case against someone perceived as having "deep pockets" when the same case against someone with an average income would be dropped. Finally, these newly wealthy students, people who in many cases never expected to have an estate worth planning for, began to be concerned with preserving and passing on their fortunes at their death.

Luckily, the man from Tacoma who wanted only to teach college had been there before them. He had gotten wealthy, he had run into these problems, and he had hired the best and most unconventional minds in the financial planning business to teach him how to manage his way to wealth. He had already learned ways of dealing with the three Goliaths now facing his students: income taxes, lawsuits, and death taxes. He began to teach them these strategies...

The man taught his students to think like the CEOs of their own corporations. He showed them how to legally and ethically reduce their taxable income, spread profits among many business entities, and use the same IRS rules that multinational companies use to protect themselves from taxation. The students also learned how to control assets without owning them, minimizing the chance of losing those assets to a lawsuit.

All the business secrets of managing wealth that the man had learned over many years were written down and put into a seminar called the Wealth Institute. The students who took this seminar and began to structure and protect their wealth asked the man to organize a time for them to get together each year and share what they had learned about being in business. The Executive Retreat was the end result.

(Continued on page 147)

128

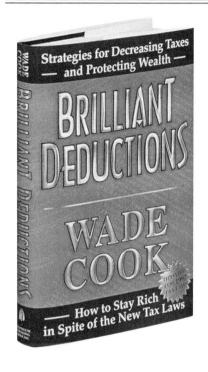

Chapter Six
Structuring Your Affairs

"There's nothing more dangerous than the U.S. Congress with an idea."

—E. Patrick McGuire of the conference Board (Opening a conference examining tax incentives)

I'm going to make two assumptions: You are either making pretty good money and want to learn how to keep more of it (for example, by saving money on taxes), or you are just starting out, either in your own business or as an investor, and you want to learn ways to structure your affairs to save money on taxes in the long run.

Either way, I'd like to start out by mentioning I believe Ronald Reagan's approach to tax reduction strategies is the best one around. His strategy summed up could be this: make more money, quit worrying about tax loop holes, quit worrying about tax shelter type investments and get on with making more money, lower the tax brackets in order to encourage people to make more.

> **Work the Brackets**

Tax Brackets

With that in mind, let's talk about the brackets and see if we can work those brackets to help you keep more. Because the tax laws are always changing, it's hard to give out the actual amounts. If you are a married person filing jointly and you're making between 0–$36,900 a year, you are going to be in a 15% tax bracket. Money made between 36,900–$89,150 a year is going to put you in a 28% tax bracket. Anything over that amount throws you into a 31–36%, and even a 39.6% bracket. I think that there is an over-looked angle to making money. It's very simple—quit making money as one entity. Instead of making money as one person, start making money as a person and a business. For example, let's say you are making around $70,000 a year. If you were making that as a sole proprietor, you would be taxed 15% on $36,900 and 28% on the remaining $33,100.

Split this money in half and make it in two different entities: a corporation making $35,000 a year is taxed in a 15% tax bracket. The other $35,000, if made yourself, is in a 15% tax bracket. Now look at what we just did. We saved 13%, which is a difference between the 15 or 28%, on the $33,100—or about $4,000 this year. And every year we can save a like amount by simply dividing up your business entities. This could be done with two different corporations, or with a sole proprietorship and a corporation, or as a person paying off fees to another corporation. There are many different angles to this.

USE DIFFERENT ENTITIES

Let me give you another angle on structuring your financial affairs. You are a company and you contract with another company to provide management, consulting, and marketing services for you or your company. You pay a fee to that company for providing these services. This is one way of moving money from one company to another, legally. Your CPA can help you structure your affairs to make sure everything is done properly. You have just lessened the tax burden in one entity by moving the money to another and paying it out as a legitimate business expense. Essentially, you are operating two different companies.

You can directly/indirectly own or control the other business enterprise. It will have a different Federal ID number, a different address, and possibly different owners (including different year-ends, et cetera).

One other point: this strategy is used extensively by companies which have corporate income tax rates based on the net profit of a corporation. Who wouldn't want to move $50,000 in expenses out of California (which taxes it at 12%) to Nevada where there is no state tax? Let me diagram this:

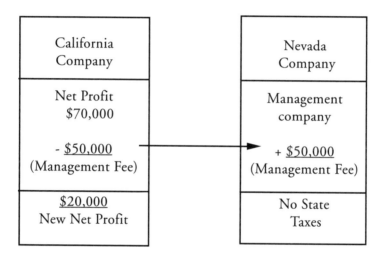

California Company	Nevada Company
Net Profit $70,000	Management company
- $50,000 (Management Fee)	+ $50,000 (Management Fee)
$20,000 New Net Profit	No State Taxes

Many people have used this tactic to convert rental income, which is not subject to social security taxes, but which, on the other hand, does not factor into the percentage of money which can go into a Pension Plan, into earned income. A person with a number of rental properties may pay out fees (rental management fees) to another company, lessening the profits on the rental properties, but putting that money into another company and making that money available for an exclusion into retirement accounts.

CAPITAL GAINS—ACTIVE OR PASSIVE

What about capital? It is either active or passive. If you bought IBM stock for $55 and sold it for $65, you made $10 per share of active capital gain. If you bought rental real estate for $150,000 and sold it for $300,000, that would be a passive capital gain. The easiest way to think about this is to relate it to two different swimming pools—the types of investment income and losses are calculated against each other. All active income and losses are calculated against each other. All passive income and losses are calculated against each other. They don't mix.

Business Calculations

A great way to save money on taxes is to have your own business, whether it is a corporation or sole proprietorship. A lot of bills can be deducted from life insurance, medical insurance, and board of directors meetings in different places around the country. I believe if you are going to be in business, you should be a corporation. Sole proprietorships are dangerous. Many people call me and are in trouble because they are vulnerable to lawsuits and have not set up a corporation.

If you are a corporation, working the tax brackets is really important. Corporations can have all kinds of expenses, and they can do a lot of things for you which you can't do for yourself.

Double Taxation

People are afraid of double taxation, which is simply this: the corporation cannot deduct dividends and the individual who receives dividends is going to have to pay taxes on that income, therefore double taxation. If the money is taken out as a salary or bonus, these are tax deductible items to the "C" corporation. There are three circumstances where you may want to consider being an "S" corporation:

1) Rental real estate

2) Small group investment

3) Any high cash-flow business (over $125,000 a year).
   [Note: If you have other losses.]

"S" corporations are very limited in what they can deduct. The best way to save money is to use your own brain power: study and research. You pay for education once, you continually pay for ignorance.

I'M NOT BIG ON 'S' CORPORATIONS

OWNERSHIP-CONTROL-INCOME

Many people who come to my seminars are worried about the implications of lawsuits and erosion of their asset values due to excessive taxation. They are worried about passing along all their assets to their children. They want to live the good life, and yet they see how exclusions by the government are going to affect them. They also realize we live in a trigger-happy lawsuit society.

There are four questions you need to ask yourself when setting up your legal entities. 1) Who is going to own them? 2) In what format are they going to own them? 3) Who is going to control the entity? 4) Who will receive the income and in what manner?

As Americans, we believe everything has to be even. We believe, if you own 50% of a company, you are entitled to 50% of that company—50% of the ownership and 50% of the cash flow. Nothing could be further from the truth. The real truth is you could own 1% of the company, control 75% and be entitled to 65% of the cash flow. Ownership, control and cash flow have nothing to do with each other.

Once you understand this concept, every time you set up a legal entity you need to ask yourself, "Who is going to own it? Who is going to control it? How will it be run? Who is going to get the income and how will it be paid out?" Realize that once you see these could be diverse percentages, all kinds of things become possible. You can literally own $^1/100$ of 1% of a company and control 100% of it. But since your ownership is so small, you could keep your estate really small, while controlling a multi-million dollar enterprise.

I ask people at my seminars, "Let's say you're worth $1 million, how much of that (what percentage) would you like put at risk to avoid losing the

You can control with very little ownership

whole thing?" Most people do not have $1 million tied up in one asset. If they are worth a million dollars, this usually involves several hundred thousand dollars in a business enterprise and perhaps several hundred thousand dollars in real estate owned by the enterprise. It may involve one or two hundred thousand dollars in brokerage accounts. Again, the question I ask is, "What percentage of this money would you like to have at risk?"

A lot of them say, "None."

You really can't say none. If you're not willing to put a small percentage of this money at risk, you risk losing the whole thing. Compare it to gangrene. If you get gangrene in your foot and you're not willing to cut off that foot, you could risk losing your leg or even your whole life. If you're not willing to risk losing a small percentage, you stand the chance of losing everything. With this in mind, I came up with Rules A and B.

Rule A

Rule A is what I call the 20% rule. Whatever your net worth is, no more than 20% of your total should be owned in one legal entity. For example, if your net worth is $1 million, you could set up some corporations. Corporation #1 would be worth $180,000—this is made by buying and selling properties. You set up corporation #2 worth $240,000. This corporation is purchasing notes and mortgages and it has interest income. You have a Limited Partnership worth $220,000. That $220,000 is the equity in rental properties. Corporation #3 is worth $160,000. This corporation is a dry cleaning business you own.

My 20% rule

Another Limited Partnership, which has some rental properties, is worth $200,000. It's never going to be exactly even because your equities and assets are going up and down in value. All this adds up to about one million dollars.

134

Out of the blue, someone comes into your dry cleaning business, gets hurt on one of your machines, and claims you are negligent. They are suing you and the insurance will not cover the damages. That corporation may be forced into bankruptcy.

Let's say the dry cleaning business was owned in your own name and somebody were to come in and sue—that little rotten apple could contaminate all the others in the bushel. You could risk losing everything because you could have liens against you from that dry cleaning business which could be attached to all of your rental real estate, your personal residence, and so on.

Rule A specifically says no more than 20% should be owned in one particular entity. Each one of these corporations has its own tax bracket; each limited partnership has the money flowing down to the different owners—which could be different from partnership to partnership.

> **DIVIDE AND CONQUER**

RULE B

Rule B is for people just starting out. First you set up one corporation, and when that corporation gets to be worth 150,000–$200,000 in investments or equities, you set up another corporation. Let's say you grow a corporation until it's worth 150,000-$200,000. You need tax write-offs at that time, but you want to own them through a Limited Partnership. A Limited Partnership would buy rental properties worth $150,000–$200,000. If you want to keep buying more, set up another Limited Partnership. You grow in leaps and bounds like this, and you do not accumulate all your wealth in one legal entity.

After following Rule A or B, and creating several, different legal entities, you could create a parent corporation. (For further explanation, see Chapter Seven.) You could have these different entities paying money to each other for providing services for each other. This is another way of moving money from one year to the next and one entity to the next, to lessen the tax bite.

Contents

from "Brilliant Deductions"

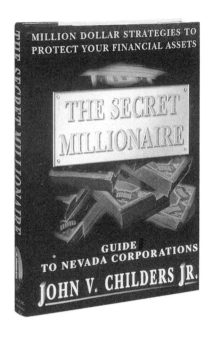

II
DECIDING ON INVISIBILITY

"Nothing will come of nothing. Dare mighty things."

SHAKESPEARE

S hould I form my own corporation? What will it help me to accomplish? How can it assist me with my particular situation? Should I do it now or later? Do you know the answer to these questions? If not, you better learn them.

These are but a few of the many questions I hear from people across the country when I speak to them about corporations. The decision to incorporate is one of the most important ones you will ever make. And it's one you *must* make in order to deal with the three areas that were covered in Chapter I.

If you do not know the answers to those questions, rest assured that you are not alone. The fact is, most people do not know the answers. However, if they can't answer those simple questions, how on earth can they consider actually forming and operating a corporation? To many people, the thought of ever having their own corporation seems like a task far too complicated. As you will see, that is certainly not the case. It's not difficult, it's just different.

The key to answering the questions lies in gaining a full understanding of exactly what it means to become incorporated. You must truly understand corporations before you decide to form one.

As you begin your endeavor of fully understanding Nevada Corporations, I believe you must first begin with the absolute basics. While studying the basics may be quite elementary for some, it has proven to be essential in gaining an in-depth comprehension of any topic, much less one as complex as a legal entity. Besides that, regardless of your level of experience, you can never get enough of the fundamentals.

Think about it. When you go to watch your favorite sports team play, when they practice before the game, are they practicing the difficult plays or the basics? The basics! If that is what the professionals do, perhaps you should take a hint and do the same thing. If you want to get the best results, you must do things in the best manner possible. Learn from those who are getting the results that you would like in your life. That is the secret applied by today's millionaires.

If you want to know about something, you first need to know what it is. With this in mind, you have to ask the most basic questions first. The most basic question to deal with when it comes to corporations is simply, "What is a corporation?" We will answer this question before going any further.

WHAT IS A CORPORATION?

If you were to ask most people to define the term "corporation," I'm quite sure you would get a myriad of responses, none of which may be correct. I'm convinced, as I travel throughout the country speaking with individuals from all walks of life, that there is a huge misconception as to exactly what it means to be incorporated.

Generally, the term conjures up images of New York City and the vast array of skyscrapers which serve as headquarters to the Fortune 500 companies. While these huge multinational companies may indeed be corporations, it must be realized that the corporation can also be the mom and pop grocery on your local street corner. It's also the real estate agency through which you purchased your home, the insurance agent you play golf with, and the restaurant where you have dinner.

Most people simply don't see these smaller businesses when they envision corporations. But in actuality, it is these smaller businesses that make up the bulk of corporations throughout the world. It is these smaller businesses which mean more to the average person when it comes to benefiting from the use of a corporation. In fact, it is these smaller businesses which belong to many of today's millionaires.

The typical corporation in this country is a small business. In many instances, this small business, this small *corporation*, is owned and operated by families and even friends. This seems strange to many people who tend to think of corporations more in terms of those companies whose shares are traded on Wall Street.

The fact is, the overwhelming vast majority of corporations in this country are privately held. Actually, of the thousands, even millions, of corporations currently operating in the United States, an extremely small number are publicly traded. The chances are, if you are reading this book with the thought of forming a corporation, you are not planning to form this type of publicly traded company. At least not yet, anyway.

This makes it a bit more difficult to explain to someone about corporations because much of what they know comes from what they have learned in conjunction with the stock market. It seems that people all too often tend to associate all corporations with the Dow Jones Industrials.

This really comes as no surprise since a good knowledge of corporations can help one develop a greater understanding of how and why stock is traded on the various exchanges. Considering that some 50 million individuals have brokerage accounts, it is not hard to see why the primary understanding of corporations comes from this arena.

A slight familiarity with corporations is inherent in any investment and/or trading environment. To truly understand corporations, and, more importantly to understand how you can benefit by having a corporation, you need to set aside any preconceptions you have and look at corporations from a whole new perspective. If you can do this, it can mean money in your pocket!

Let's begin by looking at some of the legal definitions of a corporation. Then we'll break those definitions down into language that is more understandable and readily applicable to your daily life. One of the first steps in finding out what any legal term means is to look it up in a law dictionary. The most common dictionary, *Black's Law Dictio-*

nary, defines a corporation as:

> An artificial person or legal entity created by or under authority of the laws of a state or nation, composed, in some rare instances, of a single person and his successors, being the incumbents of a particular office, but ordinarily consisting of an association of numerous individuals, who subsist as a body politic under a special denomination, which is regarded in law as having a personality and existence distinct from that of its several members, and which is by the same authority, vested with the capacity of continuous succession, irrespective of changes in its membership, either in perpetuity or for a limited term of years, and of acting as a unit or single individual in matters relating to the common purpose of the association, within the scope of the powers and authorities conferred upon such bodies by law.
>
> Dartmouth College v. Woodward, 17 U.S. (4 Wheat.) 518, 636, 657, 4 L.Ed. 629; U.S. v. Trinidad Coal Co., 137 U.S. 160, 11 S.Ct. 57, 34 L.Ed. 640.

There it is. Now, does that clear everything up for you? That is the official definition of what it means to be a corporation, straight from the Supreme Court. After reading this definition, I have a question for you: what is a corporation?

Seriously! I learned this lesson the hard way. Early on, when I was first studying to be an attorney, I met with a lady who wanted to know about a corporation. I did what I thought at the time to be the best thing which was to draft a memorandum outlining this legal definition of a corporation. Her response was certainly not what I expected but it taught me a valuable lesson. Her response was, "Everything I need to know about what it means to be a corporation is written right there in plain English but I still don't have a clue what it means." Talk about an enlightening experience. I learned right then and there that people want real world answers rather than a lot of technical legal jargon.

While this may be the legal definition of a corporation, it does little to shed light on the issue of what a corporation means to the average person. Too many times, this is exactly the case. You can go to an attorney and he can give you page after page of information on a subject and you leave the office more confused than you started, despite the fact that you actually have the "appropriate" documentation purportedly answering your questions. With this in mind, let's take a little different approach to defining exactly what it means to be a corporation.

Basically, a corporation is a separate and legal, artificial person. That's right, a separate person from you. The corporation is not you and you are not the corporation. It is completely separate, a distinct entity separate and apart from you. It has the same rights as a person but it is more of a legal entity than a person. This point needs further attention.

A corporation is a separate legal entity. It is an entity separate and apart from its members, stockholders, directors and officers. While it is indeed a separate entity, it is still dependent upon others in order to take any action. This is the best news of all.

That is great news for you because you are the person upon whom the corporation is dependent. The corporation can act only through its members, officers and directors or agents thereof. Although it is separate, the best part of this is that it can have no knowledge or belief on any subject independent of the knowledge or belief of those who control the corporation. This works very well since you are going to be the person(s) in control. It can do nothing unless you tell it to.

You are in control over this entity in the same way that a parent is in control of their children (ideally). Some of you may be thinking that this is not necessarily a good thing. You may be thinking that you've got enough on your hands with your kids without having another one when you form your corporation. The difference is that the corporation always minds you, no matter what the situation. Wouldn't that be nice? Do you understand the power in that? Let's take a closer look.

The corporation is an artificial person. Its rights, duties and liabilities do not differ from those of a natural person under like conditions. The only difference between a corporation and those directing it is that it lacks the ability to think for itself. That is the purpose of the officers and directors. These individuals do the thinking for the corporation.

To evidence this fact, documentation is kept for all decisions made on behalf of the corporation in the form of minutes and/or corporate resolutions. These documents are crucial and will be discussed in later sections in much greater detail. This distinction between the entity and those who control it becomes key in determining exactly what it is that people are searching for when they make the decision to form a corporation.

This also leads to our next question which will really be a bit more telling in understanding what a corporation is all about. It often requires more information than a simple definition of an item before your mind can form a picture of the item. The trick is to understand what that particular item does. What is the function that it performs which makes it of value to you? Knowing what it is that a corporation does will reveal more about the entity and why a person would want to have one.

For example, if someone asked you what a car is, you would be hard pressed to tell them without telling them what it does. Just as you cannot truly understand what an automobile is without knowing what it does, so it is with a corporation.

SUMMARY

The decision to form a Nevada Corporation can prove to be one of the most important decisions of your life. It is a decision to take charge of your financial situation by implementing one of the most powerful tools used by today's millionaires. Gaining a good working knowledge of the formalities and requirements of this *amazing* tool will enable you to accomplish things which most people believe to be unachievable. *It is a decision that will change your life.*

The benefits of Nevada Corporations are tremendous!
You, too, can take advantage of the tax laws that
benefit thousands of companies. Call **1-800-706-4741**
and we'll send you a FREE audio tape on *The Power
Of Nevada Corporations*!

CONTENTS
FROM "THE SECRET MILLIONAIRE"

Among all the secrets the man taught, the most important was treating the stock market or real estate like a business, both diversifying and coordinating many strategies together...

(Continued on page 163)

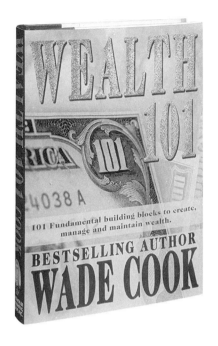

You, Inc.

When you get up in the morning and you look in the mirror you are looking at You, Inc. You're the president, the vice president, the secretary and treasurer, you're the board of directors, you're everyone. Because you are on the board of directors and you're controlling this little corporation—You, Inc.—it's very important that you understand just a few things about business.

If another company were taking over your company, when the new directors and officers show up on Monday morning they look at the balance sheets, the assets, the liabilities, they look at everything about the company. They've got to make some decisions about what they're going to keep, what they're going to help grow, what they're going to throw money into, and what they're going to try to pay off. They're going to look at your assets. They don't care when you bought something or even why you bought something. They want to know, "What is this asset producing for us? What is it making? And if we wanted to have it making more money how much more money will it take?"

Right now, you have a portfolio of stocks and bonds. You have real estate. No matter what you have, what I'd like you to do is to pretend you're doing a merger and another board of directors shows up. They

91

You, Inc.

look at your asset sheet and they say, "What is there about these holdings, investments, and assets that I would get rid of and what would I keep?" This is really tough to do, by the way, because you need to look at yourself from an outside person's point of view.

Get rid of all the emotional stuff and say, "What is producing me money and how much is it producing?" By the way, you can do this from a personal point of view, too. You can say, "I'm too sarcastic. Well, hey, that serves no purpose whatsoever. I need to get rid of that." You can get rid of some of the baggage. You can get rid of some of those things now. It's really tough to do, but you can do it if you decide to.

On the road to wealth we have to change a lot of things and the only motivational thing I'll say is that you're never going to change your bottom line until you change your head—what's in there and your attitude. It's not a complicated process.

When you see a rocket taking off, do you see that great, big tank on the back? What is that? It's fuel and it's only designed to get it a few thousand feet off the ground. Once it's out in space it takes very little fuel to run.

Remember what I said before about rockets? To get something up off the ground, let's compare it to a hot air balloon if you will. I lived in Arizona for many years. Can I share something with you that I learned about hot air balloons? I was out there watching these hot air balloons and I noticed that they only went up in Arizona in the winter time because it's so hot in the summer time. I thought at first that it must be a lot of work to launch and people don't want to work in the heat. But that's not the answer. The answer is that the hot air balloons do not go up in the summer because they need the cool air on the outside for them to rise. They need opposition. I think we're all kind of like that. We're going to have opposition. We're going to have things that we need to overcome, things that we need to do.

Life is a journey. I was retired at an early age and after being retired for seven months I realized that I really didn't like it. So, I went back out and started doing a lot more deals. There's more fun to me in the chase than in the catch.

Even now, I'm in my late 40s, and I've retired a couple of times. I could retire again, but I love teaching and I love working with people.

I love structuring people. I love teaching my Wall Street Workshop and Wealth Academy. That's what I enjoy doing. So while we're trying to overcome all these things, it's good to realize that probably a lot of us have things in our portfolio, things in our asset liability sheet that do not need to be there.

What debts can we clear up? What things can we get rid of that are holding us back? What investments do we have that we need to buy more of or get them making even more money? What can we do to improve them? So remember, regarding You, Inc. doing this pretend merger is a great exercise and I do it a couple of times a year. A couple times a year I look at everything that I have and make some decisions on some of the investments I have that are just not panning out and get rid of them. I cut my losses and get on to other things that really make a lot of money.

92

Being More, Doing More

Being more, doing more. I learned this from a friend of mine, who was also a seminar speaker. He was really big into rental type real estate and solving problems with rentals by taking on partners and by getting the tenants in the property to act more like owners of the property. He has a sentence in his seminar that I think is really powerful. He said, "Grow out of your problems." If you have a cash flow problem, buy more, create more to solve that cash flow problem. Don't cut back. If you have a tax problem, don't cut back growth. Purchase more things that will help you solve that problem.

Now a lot of us have been behind the eight ball before. We sometimes get in trouble with our businesses. They're not doing the right things, they're not making us the kind of money we want. If we really think it through and if the business is worth saving, a lot of times as we go through bad times, we come out on the other side of the eight ball a lot better off than we were before.

If you look at those kinds of things, we have to possibly let some people go or scale back on different projects—kind of regroup if you will. But when we come fighting back out, we can usually be a lot bigger and better than we were before. So grow and do more.

93

Having More Fun

This one is about doing what excites you and having more fun. One of the things that I really tried to do at my seminars is to get people to have more fun with making money. Now you go to a seminar and you get all excited. You're going to go out and buy this house and you're all excited about the potential of rental real estate and what it's going to produce for you. Or you hear about mutual funds and you want to become a really top notch stock market investor—you get really excited about that. But when you go home you're all alone. You're sitting there staring at the walls and you're saying, "Oh no, now what do I do?"

I suggest, everyone, that you get so excited about your business that you can hardly wait to get out of bed in the morning. By the way, it's pretty easy to do that in real estate. When I was doing my Money Machine I could buy a house in the morning for $86,000 and sell it by that afternoon for $94,000. I knew I was going to make $8,000 before I went to bed that night. That's exciting and it's easy to get out of bed in the morning. I love being excited about things and I love being excited about the little things in life.

People keep asking me what it is that drives me. I used to say caffeine but I gave that up awhile ago. What I enjoy is teaching; I love teaching. I define a lot of who I am by my ability to teach. I really enjoy doing adult education and I want to deliver and give them a lot of information. I love the teaching process and I think you can feel my enthusiasm for that. I love teaching, so I teach my staff. We work on training to make sure that they're doing a good job for people in structuring their entities. I'm living my ideal retirement because I'm doing what I love.

Another thing about having fun, about traveling. One of the bonus packages that we have with the Financial Fortress is information on travel. Because I travel so much, I wanted to save some money so I thought about becoming a travel agent.

I'm going to suggest to you right now that you also should become an outside travel agent. If you're going to travel, why not travel and save a lot of money? And, if you could travel and save a lot of money, how many of you would travel a lot more? Let me just share this with you about becoming a travel agent because it's fun. For your information, I've said this before and I've said it many times, if you purchase a seminar that's an investment type seminar, it's probably not tax deductible. But if you purchase a seminar for business purposes, for starting a business, for running a business, then those seminars are tax deductible.

For example, I do seminars in Hawaii a couple of times a year. Anytime you want to go to Hawaii, call my office, find out when we're doing a seminar in Hawaii, and go over there as a business seminar. All or part of that trip could be tax deductible because you're attending a business seminar in Hawaii.

Let's get back to travel. We've made arrangements with a company out of Orlando, Florida—Ideal Travel—to take people on as outside travel agents. An outside agent is not somebody sitting there with a computer all day long booking tickets and such. You operate out of your bedroom, out of your home, out of your business and you become an outside agent. You call an 800 number if you want to book tickets.

The cost is around $500 to do this, depending on whether it's a couple or just one person. For $500 to $600 you can become an outside agent. They send you training manuals and other information. Let me tell you why you should consider doing this.

First of all, you get incredible savings. Hotels and other travel companies in the industry will offer you certain courtesies to extend their business and to make sure that you're well taken care of because you're in the business. You can book tickets for other people. I stay at hotels that sometimes cost $250 night for $80 and $90 a night. I stay at $120 hotels for $40 or $50. I save about 50% on all my hotel bills almost all the time, sometimes even 70%. I used to rent cars for $40 or $50 a day now I'm renting them for $12 to $18 a day and getting upgrades from a $12 car to a Cadillac for $16.99 a day.

We have special arrangements at major theme parks. They usually allow travel agents in for free with parties of up to four people. You show your travel agent ID card and boom, you're in.

You can also save money on airline tickets. Because Ideal Travel is associated with several consolidators, they can shop for and get the very, very best tickets they can. This is not being on some travel agent's ARC (Airline Reporting Corporation) list where you get 75% off the coach fair.

It has nothing to do with that. We get a standard ordinary ticket. When you show up to the airline and you get on the plane, you get your frequent flier miles and you're paying for a ticket just like anybody else. You save money only because they'll shop for you and find the very best that they can.

Number three is that you can earn commissions—in the industry typically it is a 10% commission. So, if you have an $800 flight the commission on that would be $80 and you get half of that. You get 50% of the 10% or about $40 in this example. You're not going to get rich off of this and you'll get a 1099 form at the end of the year, but you'll get checks every few months on all the commissions that you've earned up till that point in time.

Another reason for being a travel agent is upgrades. Almost 80% of the time I fly, I buy a coach ticket and I get upgraded to first class because I'm a travel agent.

Upgrades: sometimes I come into a hotel and I've got a $35 a night a room, which is normally $120, but then they go ahead and put me in the presidential suite which is a $300 or $400 a night room for $35 or $45. I've stayed all over the place in really nice hotels and gotten upgrades. Upgrades to first class, upgrades to better cars, I mean, they really try to take care of people in the travel agent industry.

Another thing are the FAM packages. FAM stands for familiarization—technically, it's familiarization and educational packages. These companies, hotels, and airlines put together whole trips for travel agents. Some that I've been on in the past include a four day and four night trip to a brand new Radisson Hotel in Acapulco for free, a ski trip to Vail, Colorado, airfare in and out, bus tickets to Vail from Denver, four nights lodging, the whole thing for $150. And this is like a $1,500 trip that you get for $150 as a FAM package for travel agents.

My wife and I went to London. Whole trip to London, a whole week long trip to London for $459. Eight days, eight nights, airfare, everything. All we do is bring money for food. I highly recommend that you look into Ideal Travel's outside agent program.

You should become an expert at something. I read a book many years ago by a man who did research on millionaires and why they made it. I used to ask this, by the way, at my seminars. I'd say, "How many of you have made money in real estate?" Now, if there was an audience of 200 people there and people were millionaires, most of them were from real estate. A few from other kinds of investments, but most of them were from real estate.

94

Become An Expert

According to my research, and the man that wrote this book, they found out that most people that got to be worth $1 million did not do so by any form of investment, they did so by getting to be an expert in their own field.

For example, one man who was making $40,000 a year went back to college, got a masters degree and got a better job making $60,000. He then went out and got a PhD and was making $90,000 a year. When he finally got up to $120,000 a year he was still living on about $30,000 to $40,000 and he was able to put aside $60,000 to $70,000 a year into his different savings and investments.

They did research on this and found out that most of the people that were millionaires, did so by getting to be an expert in their field. They were not good at investing. Their average rate of return on their investments was 5 or 6%. Now, any one of you can just buy a better mutual fund and get 12% and 18% return. These people were not investors, they were experts in their field.

My contention is that if you could get to be an expert in a field that has a really high rate of return, for example real estate investing or some of my ideas in the stock market; if you could just narrow down the things we've done here in this book, you can go home, continue studying and get to be an expert in that field.

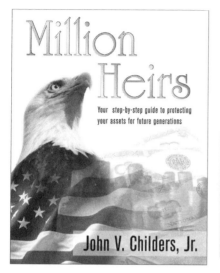

Part I
General Information

he first type of information which needs to be gathered is quite basic, but it is also often overlooked. Much of the personal information you take for granted day to day is not common knowledge to those closest to you. For instance, do you know your spouse's Social Security number? How about his or her driver's license number? You see, general information such as your address, phone number, Social Security number, and date of birth should be documented not only as it applies to you, but also to your spouse, your children, and perhaps even your grandchildren. This information and the related input forms can be found in this General Information section.

Perhaps the most important information you can document for your loved ones are the names and phone numbers of your personal and professional contacts and advisors. Too many times, individuals tend to forget about those who will be playing a key role in the handling of their estates and the accompanying circumstances. You need to put together a listing of all these key players. Having this valuable resource close at hand could prove invaluable to those who will eventually have to close your estate.

You may think that this is a simple matter because there really aren't that many people involved, but you may be quite surprised. Think about it. Think about all the people who are involved in your day-to-day affairs. The following is just a short list of some of the central figures.

Minister/Rabbi/Priest: Many people tend to forget to include instructions for how they want their funeral handled. What's more, they forget to tell who they want to preside over the ceremony. Your personal or family minister is most likely the one who will be asked to do the eulogy at your funeral. For this reason, it is crucial to have this information available for those you leave behind.

Insurance Agent: Your insurance agent will undoubtedly need to be contacted in order to access your life insurance information. In many instances, family members may not be familiar with who provides your insurance. It may be a close friend of yours, but your children may have never met this person. It is important to have this person identified for those handling your affairs. Additionally, as you will see while assembling this information, there could be several individuals who would need to be contacted regarding life or accidental death insurance.

Attorney: The role of your attorney(s) is a matter of great importance in settling your estate. Your attorney(s) will have all relevant information regarding your will, trusts, estate plans, pending legal matters, and other vital records and documents. Because they play such a large part in this process, it is especially important to document all names, numbers, and addresses.

Accountant: The role of the accountant in the overall process is extremely important. Upon your death, there are a number of issues which must be addressed regarding your tax situation and possibly, obligation. Your accountant will have copies of all previously filed income tax returns, as well as pertinent tax strategies you have put into practice.

Stockbroker: Many times, individuals may have established investment and trading accounts that others are not aware of. Your broker will have information on your investment portfolio. However, this does you no good whatsoever unless you list the name of each broker and how to get into contact with them.

Financial Planner: A profession which plays a larger part today than ever before in the estate planning and financial planning process is the financial planner. Your personal financial planner will have details on all of your investments, retirement plans, insurance policies, and estate plans.

Realtor: Your realtor could be needed in the event your heirs wish to sell your current home. In many instances, this becomes increasingly important in order to satisfy any obligations surrounding the estate. It can save a lot of time, effort, energy, and even money, by having the name of a trusted advisor to assist in this matter rather than searching for just anyone.

Doctor: Upon the death of an individual, various records are needed for many different purposes. One set of these records is those documenting your medical history. This can be required for many different reasons including insurance, et cetera. Your medical specialists will have your medical history documented and can provide this information upon demand. These medical specialists can include, but are not limited to, your family practitioner, dentist, pediatrician, OB/GYN, and ophthalmologist.

Veterinarian: Your veterinarian will have the shot records and medical information on your pets. This may not seem necessary, but can be quite helpful when folks pass away leaving pets behind for family members to take care of.

This is but a small listing of the various individuals who will play a key role in the overall handling of your estate. Input forms for the contacts and advisors listed above, as well as space for other contacts, can be found in the following pages. Be sure to fill these out completely and to keep them up to date as the years go by.

Excerpt From "Million Heirs"

Family Information

	You	**Spouse**
Name		
Address Street/PO Box		
City/State Zip Code		
Social Security #		
Date of Birth		
Place of Birth		
Occupation		
Place of Employment Company Name Street/PO Box		
City/State Zip Code		
Employer's Phone #		
Driver's License #		
Parent's Name		
Parent's Phone #		

Child 1   **Child 2**

Name _____   _____

Address _____   _____
Street/PO Box _____ _____

City/State _____   _____
Zip Code _____   _____
Phone # _____   _____

Social Security # _____ _____

Date of Birth _____   _____
Place of Birth _____ _____
Parent's Name _____   _____

Child 3   **Child 4**

Name _____   _____

Address _____   _____
Street/PO Box _____ _____

City/State _____   _____
Zip Code _____   _____
Phone # _____   _____

Social Security # _____ _____

Date of Birth _____   _____
Place of Birth _____ _____
Parent's Name _____   _____

Contents

from "Million Heirs"

SECTION 4

The Dream Continues

The man's students wholeheartedly embraced his business strategies. The success of his new books and seminars based on entities and wealth management blossomed. But still there was one part of the picture that even some of his most successful students and business partners resisted—preparing their estate and their affairs for the inevitable future.

Started with only $3,000 and a promise not to hire anyone else, the man's company now has over 500 employees and 27 subsidiaries. It is a publicly traded company on the over-the-counter bulletin board market. There are over 25,000 graduates of the Wall Street Workshop, many of whom have made enough money in the stock market within two years to retire from their jobs.

Most of these successful people have shared one primary trait—the drive to keep learning more about business and stock market principles and strategies. The ever-increasing demand for more training has led to more and more books and seminars, many of them developed by the man's most successful students who have become speakers and trainers for his company.

(*Continued on page 181*)

163

EXPLANATIONS

NEWSLETTER

CONTINUING EDUCATION FOR GENERATING CASH FLOW

A PUBLICATION OF THE AMERICAN NEWSLETTER COMPANY

Success is a never-ending project. You may have the motivation, drive, knowledge and skill to achieve your goals now, but to maintain your edge over time it is extremely important to keep on learning. For those who wish to succeed financially, *EXPLANATIONS* Newsletter provides focused, continuing education that will keep you sharp and constantly ready for action. Every month of the year, *EXPLANATIONS* brings you timely, informative articles covering wide variety of financial issues with the aim of helping you increase your profits and ultimately improve the lives of you and your loved ones. Tell us your questions; we'll give you complete *EXPLANATIONS*...

February

High Octane Options

By Steve Wirrick

Conventional wisdom on Wall Street says, "the trend is your friend." Although this sounds simplistic, I have found it a powerful adage to follow. My approach to identify the trend is mostly technical. I'm a visual person, so I like looking at charts. I can see who's winning the battle between the bulls and the bears and stay on the right side of the trade.

Seeing the trend lets me buy and sell with confidence. The nice thing about charts is that there are clear patterns you can learn to recognize. We cover several in the **High Octane Options** seminar. One of my favorite patterns is the rectangle, used in other Wade Cook seminars to identify Rolling Stock. I roll the options. But what I really love is when the stock breaks out of its trading range. Huge price moves often result, and huge profits can follow.

Another thing I check to identify the trend is volume—the number of shares traded. If volume starts increasing at the same time prices do, even higher prices could come. A great example of this is a trade I did on Zitel Corp. (ZITL). Right after it split in December of 1996, I saw prices climbing higher, and volume started to expand. When the stock was at $30, I bought the March $25 calls for $9.25. Ten days later I sold at $40.88. All because I keyed into volume . . .

EXPLANATIONS

March

Take a Bite... Out of Taxes

By Dan Fitzpatrick

I am always gratified when I can help someone to legally, morally, and ethically reduce their tax burden through proper use of entities such as limited partnerships, corporations, and pension plans. Occasionally, though, I run into someone who doesn't get it. While they resent paying excessive taxes, they feel uncomfortable paying less. It's as if they have been playing on an uneven field for so long that a level playing field just doesn't feel right

to them. They seem to think that the laws providing for the formation of these entities apply only to the "rich and famous." In fact, these opportunities exist for all of us, and we ignore them at our financial peril . . .

April

Speaker's Soapbox: Positive Puts

By Richard Williams Simmons

Since we are trading in a highly volatile market where the trend can be up or down at any given time, we need to have enough tools in our toolbox to take

care of whatever job we face and increase our chances to succeed. We do this by giving ourselves alternative actions for when a stock does not perform the way we expect it to. Though the strategy I'm about to outline, like all successful option trading, requires some diligence, it allows you to put in place some "hooks" to protect your position.

When trading options, we like to work with an underlying stock that has a fair amount of volatility, so we look for a beta of 1.3 or greater (see Back to Basics on page 7 for more information about beta). This higher "implied" volatility prompts the market makers to price the options attractively for us. Trying this strategy on a relatively flat stock may not achieve the desired results.

Here's an example of this powerful strategy using Citicorp (CCI). On November 25, 1997, Citicorp like many other stocks was battling back after the October downturn. The stock opened at $120, hit a high of $120 15/16, a low of $117 1/2, and closed at $119 1/4. The stock was in a definite downtrend, but the main question is, would the trend continue, and for how long? Should we buy a call? Should we buy a put? At what strike price? When I have these questions, I frequently buy the closest strike price put. In this particular case, I felt that the best investment would be to buy the December $120 put. But considering the recent volatility, compared to longer term rising trend, might a long-term call be warranted? By buying a put instead, I effectively double my chances of winning on this particular trade.

First, if the stock continues its downward trend, I would hold the put as a long position and then sell it for a profit. (Remember that buying gives me the right but not the obligation to do something.) On the other hand, if the stock reverses direction and becomes bullish, I will sell the December $125 put. What I have done is create a Bull Put Spread, sometimes known as a Put Credit Spread, one leg at a time. Here is the scenario:

Bought: December $120 puts at $1.50

Sold: December $125 puts at $3.125

I created a $5 spread ($125 minus $120) and put $1 5/8 income into my account ($3 1/8 in minus $1 1/2 out = $1 5/8 credit). We now have the profits from selling, as Wade emphasizes, and have covered our "naked" put position.

Now, how will this Bull Put Spread play out? ...

Get monthly coaching, training, motivation and education.
Call today to put *EXPLANATIONS* in your corner!
1-800-706-2825

Appendix One

A Letter From Wade Cook

The following is a letter (advertisement) I sent to people at about the time my book, "Wall Street Money Machine" was near completion. I wanted to share with you information about the Wall Street Workshop and could think of no better way than to include a copy of the letter here. My life is dynamic. Things are always changing, so to find out current schedules, tuition and dates—plus an update of topics covered at the event, please call 1–800–872–7411.

Tuition and schedule are subject to change without notice.

> *"The Wade Cook seminar (Wall Street Workshop) is a serious, no hype, intense, brain-swelling experience! In my opinion, this is an absolute must for anyone who thinks he knows what he is doing with regard to making money in the stock market. This is an "eye-opening" experience that makes me, who I considered to be an experienced trader, feel like I have never really made a good deal, even though I have hundreds of thousands of dollars invested in the market. They say that you can make back your seminar fee if you are not afraid to move on their strategies. I had my doubts before getting there. I no longer have any doubts. The first day, I made back my fee and much more—over $3,000. The actual return on my investment was 26% in a single day. If you work for your money, this seminar is a must. You'll learn you won't have to work for much longer!"*
>
> —Don G.

Cash Flow and Beyond

Dear Friend,

My name is Wade Cook. I made a fortune in real estate and then wrote a book about it: *Real Estate Money Machine*. Since then I've traveled to 43 states, been interviewed on over 1,600 radio and TV talk shows, and have spoken to millions of people. My theme has been cash flow and retiring rich.

That first book changed the way thousands of people handled real estate. *Real Estate Money Machine* (and 17 other books I've written) has been successful, and my seminar career has been super successful. I then put some of my profits into the stock market with dismal results, but after years of trying and exploring, I stumbled across a few ways of making money— actually _making really great money_. I'd like to invite you to come and spend a few days at the Wall Street Workshop with me or my excellent instructors so you, too, can employ these cash- flow stock techniques.

Let me use that last sentence to tell you what my style of investing entails. There are three reasons and benefits to investing: cash flow, tax write-offs, and growth. The most important is cash flow. Your need for tax write-offs and growth will change from year to year. Your need for income will _always increase_. Also, if you learn how to create a large cash flow you can buy all the boring investments you want—later.

When I die I want my tombstone to say Wade "Cash Flow" Cook. Now, the income I'm talking about is perpetual: month after month. It's not an increase in your portfolio value, but actual cash hitting your account, a check in your mailbox.

> *"I bought 15,000 shares of Televideo at 3/8 and sold them about a week later at 3/4, doubling my money. I made $5,000 in one week!"*
> —*Wallace J.*

> *"Wow! What a ride! I netted over $3,500 in just two days _during_ the workshop. Not bad, considering I had only set up my account a few weeks before. But that is only half the story: thanks to both the workshop and the timely information I get off the W.I.N. network, I have since consistently realized returns from 5% to 25% per month."*
> —*D.B.*

170

A Letter From Wade Cook

Let's reason together: If you have your own business and you don't show up, how long will it last without you? (Across the board in America, it's $2^1/2$ weeks.) If you work for someone else, and you don't go to work, when does your income stop? You've heard of income producing assets, and for most people _they are it_. They are the only income producing asset they have, and if their asset doesn't show up for work, there's no income.

Question: Can you have income without assets? No, someone or something has to be producing the income. Next question: Can you have assets without income? Yes, and far too many of you have far too many of these: Assets with no income.

From the beginning of my financial educational career, some 16 years ago, I've been successfully helping people build up a group of assets which produces the income they need to live on: _income_ which will let them spend more time with the kids or grandkids, _income_ to go fishing, _income_ to go back and take worthwhile classes, _income_ to live the life they really want to live.

> _"From the covered call technique Wade taught today, I invested $3,937.50 and captured $750 worth of premiums in minutes. This is a 19% return for one phone call. Try it. It works! The stock is still in my account and so is the $750."_
>
> _—David S._

I love teaching, and so do my "Team Wall Street" instructors. These instructors, hand picked, are part of my investment "Mastermind" group. Several years ago I started sharing some of my stock market insights at my real estate seminars and my asset protection and entity structuring events. This led to a full-scale stock market seminar. We call it the "Wall Street Workshop."

The tuition is cheap compared to the money you'll make. It truly is a great value. Don't come if you want us to sell you investments. We don't do that. We teach unique, yet powerful _cash-flow formulas_. We treat the stock market like a business. We teach you how to get consistent one month returns of 20% to 40%. This last statement is no joke. Many people are very pleasantly surprised when they come and make those returns _right in class_.

Cash Flow and Beyond

The Wall Street Workshop is a two-day event. It is not a seminar, but a roll-up-your-sleeves and "do the deals" workshop. Team Wall Street instructors will use newspapers, charting services, brokers on the phone, etc. to not only tell you how to make money, but show you how to do it, and then _watch over you while you do it yourself._ Our format is unique in this world of "money making" events. We call it "experiential learning." You learn best by doing. We teach a formula, then we implement it. We make money in class. You, as an attendee, use the phones in the hallway (or use mobile phones), call your brokers, and make deals also. It is education at its powerful best. Read what our students learn and do:

> *"I opened an IRA account seven days ago. Using the concepts Wade teaches in the Wall Street Workshop, I bought $22,238 of stock and wrote covered calls that paid me $1,920. That is a return of 8.6%! If I am called out before the April expiration date, I will make another $2,200. That will be a five-week return of 18.5%! Annualized, that's 222%!"*
> —Verne D.

> *"This is the third time I have attended the Wall Street Workshop. Each time I learned more and more. In class, I bought 500 leaps for approximately $2,600. In one month I made over a 100% return on my investment."*
> —Tony T.

> *"This workshop became a family affair for us. We are making money in our real estate turnaround business from ideas we acquired from Wade Cook. Our surplus money will now be invested in the stock market to enable us to rapidly multiply our money and to receive cash flow and steady income. Our son and my wife established an account prior to attending the workshop. As a result of the techniques we learned, we invested in three companies, buying shares on margin. Our son instructed our broker to write covered calls on all three stocks we purchased. We invested $3,000 and will see a $1,400 return if the June calls come through. We believe that Wade Cook is a very intelligent, well-educated person who has personally acquired knowledge on how to organize business entities that enable a person to protect the income that comes from Wade Cook's creative techniques.*

A Letter From Wade Cook

This has been a great experience for us."
—*Hal, Jackie, & Rick H.*

And the most common comment we receive is that the money they made *more than paid for the tuition.*

> *"I bought $10,000 worth of stock and made $2,500 on the deal. I paid for the workshop with one trade. I plan to make much more. The seminar was invaluable."*
> —*Ray C.*

> *"I enjoyed this and learned very much. I made my investment back in the seminar by placing three trades. It was great and Wade did impress me, which is not easy!"*
> —*Mark D.*

The major point of this: If you spend your money for this invaluable information (less with tuition discounts—see end of letter) and make all of it back plus some, or even half of it, in just two days (starting with as little as a few thousand dollars to invest), then how much more will you make over the next year? This is the first event which will cost you $100,000 or more to **NOT** attend.

> *"I started with $40,000 and have made over $75,000 in the last four months since the Wall Street Workshop."*
>
> —*Barbara S.*

> *"I now have $45,000 in my account. I started with $10,000 and have made $35,000 in just over three months."*
> —*Adam C.*

The Wall Street Workshop is heavy-duty; there is no namby-pamby, wishy-washy information taught here. We teach and implement industrial-strength strategies.

And you know what? These methods are tried and proven and some are easy enough to do in an IRA.

173

Cash Flow and Beyond

Look at a brief list of the topics:

- **GETTING STARTED**
    - Strategies of Engagement
    - 5-step Process of Wealth
    - Trading Basics
    - Trading Criteria
    - Making Effective Decisions
    - Return/Yield Calculation

- **ROLLING STOCK**
    - Rolling options

- **OPTIONS**
    - Vocabulary
    - L.E.A.P.S.
    - Options/News
    - Gathering Information
    - How to Avoid Losses in Options

- **STOCK SPLITS**
    - Basics and Straight Stock Play

- **WRITING COVERED CALLS**
    - Definition
    - The Wade Cook Covered Call Formula
    - Three Rules of Covered Call Writing

- **SELLING PUTS**
    - Tandem Plays
    - Stacking the Deck in Your Favor
    - Knowing When To Sell

- **PEAKS AND SLAMS**
    - Dead Cat Bounce

- **BOTTOM FISHING**
    - News Issues
    - Spin-offs
    - Turnarounds
    - Penny Stocks

- **TAX WISE INVESTING**
  - Section 42
  - Entity Structures
  - Section 29
  - Retire Rich

There is no way a short letter can do justice, I can't begin to tell you how powerful this event is. Just think: two days of learning and implementing these "profit-charged" cash-flow formulas. You'll see example after example of deals that work. You'll work the formulas. You'll learn how to double your money every 2^1/2 to 4 months. We do it all the time. I'd like to say that the Wall Street Workshop is the _greatest event_ of its kind—_it's number one;_ BUT when I look around, no one is in second place. There is, simply put, no other format like it. We've taken the best cash-flow enhancement strategies and put them to work. Here's what you won't get at the event:

- You won't hear about mutual funds—too boring.
- You won't be sold investments; you get to keep all the profits you earn.
- You won't be bored—this is a jam-packed, "do the deals" action workshop.

You can't afford to miss this event. Even if I charged $25,000 you'd still get your _money's worth_ and more. I have a "meter drop" personality from my taxi-driving days. It has served me well in real estate and the stock market (make a killing at small, repetitive transactions), so I'll continue to use it in my educational events. I've kept the price low so _more people_ can get exposed to these _income generation strategies_.

> _"Mr. Cook has a terrific personality. I am dyslexic and understand live performance, comedy, acting, and numbers. Wade made the numbers come alive and the concepts become real. His analogies were fun to realize. If he can teach me, then he can teach anyone."_
>
> —_Toni A._

> _Wade Cook is the first person I have heard/met who thinks the same way I do. I have had questions addressed and answered by Wade that I have not been able to get answers to for 15 to 20 years. Thank you, Wade."_
>
> —_Vern V._

Cash Flow and Beyond

"I can't say enough about how much value I received from the Wall Street Workshop. I would highly recommend this workshop to anybody who wants to improve his trading skills."

—Al S.

Wade Cook Seminars, Inc. (a division of Wade Cook Financial Corporation), a company I took public awhile ago, is one sponsor of the Wall Street Workshop. Call them for seating availability (1-800-872-7411). These events are sold out constantly.

You have to ask yourself these questions: If I don't go to the Wall Street Workshop, where can I learn to take $20,000 and have it generate **$5,000 to $7,000** income per **MONTH**?
- Where can I learn to get tax credits in the stock market?
- Who else will teach me how to power up my IRA or pension plans to get 10% to 20% monthly returns—actual cash?
- Where will I go to learn to double my money every $2^1/2$ to 4 months?
- Who else is teaching?
- Options on stock split companies
- Covered call writing
- Rolling stocks
- Dividend capturing
- Short sells with hedges
- Tax structuring
- Asset protection vehicles like Pensions, Living Trusts, Nevada Corporations, Charitable Remainder Trusts, and Family Limited Partnerships.

This Wall Street Workshop is dynamic, powerful, comprehensive, innovative, yet safe and sane. You'll be angry at your stockbroker for not showing you these "easy-to-implement" formulas and strategies. I hope you come and visit with my staff, my Team Wall Street Instructors.

"Better education than any college or university. This information truly is what they don't teach you at Harvard."
—D.J.

A Letter From Wade Cook

"Rolling stocks are fantastic! With Wade's example on Amax Gold (AU), I made thousands and thousands."

—Alan R.

"The Wall Street Workshop is one of the most positive experiences I've had in class in a long time. It is great to have a class where you have access to current data rather than historical trends."

—Patricia H.

"We have been investing in the market for a long time. We have been making excellent profits, but Wade Cook gave us additional information that would benefit us and greatly increase our profits. Most people cannot challenge your thinking, but Wade Cook makes your mind come alive. Thank you, Wade. You are always great!"

—Mary D.

The low tuition is a *true value* in and of itself, and I'll *even give a guarantee*: 3 Trades, 3 Months, 300% Return! Team Wall Street shall find, during your **Wall Street Workshop**, or within three months afterwards, at least three transactions earning a 300% annualized return. The transactions will be listed on **W.I.N.**, the **Wealth Information Network**™ available through our website. You must be a subscriber to access **W.I.N.** If we don't show you the deals, you get your **Wall Street Workshop** tuition back.

I'm so confident of our ability to help you make money that I can make this incredible offer. I'm not saying 3% or 30% but 300%. That's THREE TIMES your money. I'll always give you back more than you give me. And again your cash flow keeps coming in, month after month. This guarantee is designed to make you successful. If you'll do what I teach, you'll make a lot of money. Where else can you get a 300% money back guarantee? Call and get registered right away.

BONUSES:

#1　This course needs no incentive, but for a very limited time I'm going to throw in a travel credit. I know you may have to travel to one of our regional events. This will help with the airfare and hotel rooms.

Clash Flow and Beyond

#2   We'd like your spouse (business partner, child) to come with you. I'll knock off a bunch and get them in at a great discount (one spouse/partner with one full, paid tuition.)

#3   I'll give you a discount to W.I.N., our 24-hours-a-day, seven-days-a-week computer information service available through our website. You can _find out_ what Team Wall Street and I are doing and do the same deals, if you like.

#4   For a very, very short time, and at certain cities, I'm going to chip in money from Wade Cook Seminar's scholarship fund. This will reduce the tuition even further. It is peanuts compared to what you'll receive. Call 1–800–872–7411 and ask for the special tuition price and scholarship.

#5   I'll also throw in a $500 discount certificate off the full price of the processing fee of a Nevada Corporation, or other legal entity set up by Wade Cook Seminars, Inc.

#6   Plus, I'll give a special discount off the **Wall Street Workshop Library Video** (a two-day taped seminar, valued at $2,995). If you can't attend, call about this video presentation, a great value also.

#7   And, if you attend the **Wall Street Workshop** soon, I'll include, free of charge, the **Business and Entity Skills Training** (B.E.S.T.) **Workshop**, which is held the day after the **Wall Street Workshop**.

All of this for a small price. I want every dollar you pay my company to come back to you tenfold. We're geared up for success. We want to share all we do with you.

> *"The Wall Street Workshop is learning to play on a higher level. It stretches the imagination. It makes us reach—but with excitement! Wade gives you the desire to reach for the moon and then he gives you the rocket to get there."*
> —*Nick and Judy D.*

> *"The last day of the seminar we made approximately $3,500 by writing covered calls"*
> —*Rudy K.*

> *"I personally think this Wall Street Workshop is great! I learned strategies that I have never heard of. I made two deals in one day. I'll gain about $1,500 on an $8,000 investment. On the other deal, I'll make about $950 on a $9,000 investment. This would have been higher if I would have used my margin account."*
>
> —*Vinh T.*

Of all the <u>*financial stepping stones*</u> in life, this workshop <u>*is a must*</u>. You'll make more, you'll keep more, you'll enhance your wealth and your cash flow. We never promise what we can't deliver and we always deliver more than we promise.

Hope to see you soon.

Sincerely Yours,

Wade B. Cook

> *"During the two days I spent in Wade Cook's workshop, I found the best structured class ever! My mind felt like it was in total meltdown and nothing was being retained until someone asked me a question on how something was done and I heard myself explaining it! Wow, I really did learn all they taught at the class!"*
>
> –*Millie L.*

> *"This workshop is exhilarating. I laughed, I cried, I went through every human emotion from birth to death. Don't miss the workshop!"*
>
> –*Ken Z.*

Call 1–800–872–7411 for dates, cities, and seating. Space is very limited, so call right away.

These courses build on the foundation of the Wall Street Workshop, the Real Estate Money Machine, and the Wealth Institute

As important as continuing education is to successful business people, continuous support and reinforcement is just as vital. The man listened to his students and developed programs and services to provide this support. Some of these services have been in place for years, and some are fairly new...

The man and his company, Wade Cook Financial Corporation, made over $100 million in 1997. And this is all from a modest dream to teach people that they can succeed, right where they are now, if they will only do what it takes to get the appropriate education and apply what they have learned. The story and the dream continue today and beyond, and now you can add your own financial success to the story. Buy one of the many books excerpted here or call about the Wall Street Workshop. Join Wade Cook, the cabbie who now drives a Bentley, for the ride of your life to the riches *you've* dreamed of, and we'll see you in the Winner's Circle with the other CEOs!